italian

...made simple

This edition published in 2011
LOVE FOOD is an imprint of Parragon Books Ltd

Parragon Publishing
Queen Street House
4 Queen Street
Bath BA1 1HE, UK

www.parragon.com

ISBN: 978-1-4454-4444-4

Printed in China

Produced by Ivy Contract
Cover design by Talking Design

Notes for the Reader

This book uses imperial, metric, and US cup measurements. Follow the same units of measurement throughout; do not mix imperial and metric. All spoon measurements are level: teaspoons are assumed to be 5 ml, and tablespoons are assumed to be 15 ml. Unless otherwise stated, milk is assumed to be whole, eggs and individual vegetables, such as potatoes, are medium, and pepper is freshly ground black pepper.

The times given are an approximate guide only. Preparation times differ according to the techniques used by different people and the cooking times may also vary from those given as a result of the type of oven used. Optional ingredients, variations, or serving suggestions have not been included in the calculations.

Recipes using raw or very lightly cooked eggs should be avoided by infants, the elderly, pregnant women, convalescents, and anyone with a chronic condition. Pregnant and breast-feeding women are advised to avoid eating peanuts and peanut products. People with nut allergies should be aware that some of the prepared ingredients used in the recipes in this book may contain nuts. Always check the package before use.

Vegetarians should be aware that some of the prepared ingredients used in the recipes in this book may contain animal products. Always check the package before use.

Picture Acknowledgements
The publisher would like to thank the following for permission to reproduce copyright material on the front cover: Fish Ravioli/Prima Press © Getty Images

italian

introduction

At the heart of Italian cuisine lies a very special ingredient—the legendary Italian love of good things, including good food. Learning the skills of cooking begins at an early age, as recipes and techniques are handed down the generations, and so too does an appreciation of well-prepared meals, whether a plate of al dente pasta topped with a simple sauce of freshly picked, sun-ripened tomatoes, a slow-cooked, aromatic beef stew, or a perfect seafood risotto.

It is often said that the essence of Italian cooking can be summed up in two words—seasonal and regional. Italians respect their ingredients and insist on the best quality, so they prefer to use seasonal produce that, if possible, is locally grown. In provincial towns and villages, people shop daily for fresh produce in the markets and plan the day's menu around whatever ingredients look, feel, and smell to be in peak condition.

This emphasis has had a lasting effect on the style of Italian cuisine, and simplicity is the key word. But simplicity means something different in each region of Italy. The reason for this is a mix of geographical and cultural diversity. The north of the country is cooler and wetter, while the south is hotter and drier, and the crops reflect this. In the north, dairy farming produces butter, cream, and cheese, which feature widely in the region's traditional cooking, and both rice and maize are cultivated here, so risotto and polenta are staples. The south, on the other hand, is the home of pasta, olives and olive oil, tomatoes, eggplants, and citrus fruits.

The cultural differences arise from the fact that Italy has only relatively recently become a unified "country," created from a number of independent states each with their own traditions, to which they adhere fiercely. This is perhaps part of the irresistible appeal of Italian cuisine—but whatever the reason, embrace it and enjoy it!

starters, soups & salads

artichokes with seafood

ingredients

serves 6

4–6 small young globe artichokes
juice of 2 lemons
$\frac{1}{4}$ cup olive oil
3 garlic cloves, sliced
$\frac{1}{2}$ cup white wine
1 lb/450 g frozen, pre-cooked
   mixed seafood (thawed)
10$\frac{1}{2}$ oz/300 g buffalo
   mozzarella, sliced
butter, for greasing
salt and pepper

method

1 Butter a baking dish. Clean the artichokes, cut the stems to a length of 1$\frac{1}{2}$ inches/4 cm, and peel. Remove the tough, outer leaves and slice off the thistles from the inner leaves.

2 Fill a bowl with 4 cups of water and add the lemon juice. Cut the artichokes lengthwise into thin slices and immediately drop them into the lemon water. Let them soak for 10 minutes, then pour off the water and drain well.

3 Heat the olive oil in a nonstick pan and fry the garlic until golden brown, then remove and discard it.

4 Sauté the artichoke slices in the olive oil, stirring constantly. Season with salt and pepper, then add the white wine. Cover the pan and gently braise the artichokes on medium heat for about 30 minutes, shaking the pan several times as they cook.

5 Place the artichoke slices in the prepared baking dish and pour on the cooking juices. Add the seafood to the artichokes and top with mozzarella slices. Bake in a preheated oven, 400°F/200°C, for 20 to 25 minutes, until the mozzarella melts and starts to brown. Serve the dish immediately.

country-style marinated eggplant slices

ingredients

serves 6

4 eggplants
6 tomatoes
2 garlic cloves
$\frac{1}{2}$ bunch parsley
$\frac{1}{4}$ cup olive oil, plus extra
for greasing
salt and pepper

method.

1 Wash and trim the eggplants, then cut into slices $\frac{1}{2}$ inch/1 cm thick. Salt them and place in a sieve to drain for 1 hour.

2 Meanwhile, peel and quarter the tomatoes, remove the seeds, and finely dice the flesh. Peel the garlic and mince it along with the parsley. Add this mixture to the tomatoes, then add salt and pepper to taste. Stir in 2 tablespoons of the olive oil and let everything marinate briefly.

3 Rinse and pat the eggplant slices dry with paper towels and arrange them next to each other on an oiled baking sheet. Drizzle the remaining olive oil over them, then roast in a preheated oven, 400°F/200°C, for 5 minutes on each side.

4 Brush the eggplant slices with the tomato mixture and stack them up into little towers before serving.

fennel salami carpaccio

ingredients

serves 4

2 large fennel bulbs
3½ oz/100 g fennel salami,
    thinly sliced

dressing
juice of 1 lemon and 1 orange
1 tsp flower blossom honey
1 tsp mustard
1 tbsp white wine vinegar
¼ cup olive oil
salt and pepper

method

1 Trim the fennel and slice it very thin, with a mandolin or a food slicer. Decoratively arrange the sliced salami and fennel on four plates.

2 Whisk together the dressing ingredients and pour over the fennel salami carpaccio. Marinate for 10 minutes or longer before serving.

parma ham & figs

ingredients

serves 4

6·oz/175 g Parma ham,
     thinly sliced
4 fresh figs
1 lime
2 fresh basil sprigs
pepper

method

1 Using a sharp knife, trim the visible fat from the slices of Parma ham and discard. Arrange the Parma ham on four large serving plates, loosely folding it so that it falls into decorative shapes. Season to taste with pepper.

2 Using a sharp knife, cut each fig lengthwise into four wedges. Arrange a fig on each serving plate. Cut the lime into 6 wedges, then place a wedge on each plate and reserve the others. Remove the leaves from the basil sprigs and divide among the plates. Cover with plastic wrap and let chill in the refrigerator until ready to serve.

3 Just before serving, remove the plates from the refrigerator and squeeze the juice from the remaining lime wedges over the ham.

variation

Drizzle 3 tablespoons of balsamic vinegar and a little extra virgin olive oil over the salad.

prosciutto with arugula

ingredients

serves 4

4 oz/115 g arugula
1 tbsp lemon juice
3 tbsp extra virgin olive oil
8 oz/225 g prosciutto,
    thinly sliced
salt and pepper

method

1 Separate the arugula leaves, wash in cold water, and pat dry on paper towels. Place the leaves in a bowl.

2 Pour the lemon juice into a small bowl and season to taste with salt and pepper. Whisk in the olive oil, then pour the dressing over the arugula leaves and toss lightly so they are evenly coated.

3 Carefully drape the prosciutto in folds on individual serving plates, then add the dressed arugula. Serve at room temperature.

chicken crostini

ingredients

serves 4

12 slices French bread
   or rustic bread
¼ cup olive oil
2 garlic cloves, chopped
2 tbsp finely chopped fresh
   oregano
3½ oz/100 g cold roast chicken,
   cut into small, thin slices
4 tomatoes, sliced
12 thin slices of goat cheese
12 black olives, pitted and chopped
salt and pepper
fresh red and green salad greens,
   to serve

method

1 Put the bread under a broiler, preheated to medium, and lightly toast on both sides. Meanwhile, pour the olive oil into a bowl and add the garlic and oregano. Season with salt and pepper and mix well. Remove the toasted bread slices from the broiler and brush them on one side only with the oil mixture.

2 Place the bread slices, oiled sides up, on a cookie sheet. Put some sliced chicken on top of each one, followed by a slice of tomato. Divide the slices of goat cheese between them, then top with the chopped olives.

3 Drizzle over the remaining oil mixture and transfer to a preheated oven, 350°F/180°C. Bake for about 5 minutes, or until the cheese is golden and starting to melt. Remove from the oven and serve on a bed of fresh red and green salad leaves.

warm vegetable medley

ingredients

serves 6–8

¼ cup olive oil
2 celery stalks, sliced
2 red onions, sliced
1 lb/450 g eggplant, diced
1 garlic clove, finely chopped
5 plum tomatoes, chopped
3 tbsp red wine vinegar
1 tbsp sugar
3 tbsp green olives, pitted
2 tbsp capers
salt and pepper
ciabatta or panini, to serve

method

1 Heat half the olive oil in a large, heavy-bottom pan. Add the celery and onions and cook over low heat, stirring occasionally, for 5 minutes, until softened but not colored. Add the remaining oil and the eggplant. Cook, stirring frequently, for about 5 minutes, until the eggplant starts to color.

2 Add the garlic, tomatoes, vinegar, and sugar, and mix well. Cover the mixture with a circle of waxed paper and let simmer gently for about 10 minutes.

3 Remove the waxed paper, stir in the olives and capers, and season to taste with salt and pepper. Pour the vegetables into a serving dish and set aside to cool to room temperature. Serve with ciabatta or panini.

sicilian stuffed tomatoes

ingredients

serves 4

8 large, ripe tomatoes
generous ¼ cup extra virgin
     olive oil
2 onions, finely chopped
2 garlic cloves, crushed
2 cups fresh breadcrumbs
8 anchovy fillets in oil, drained
     and chopped
3 tbsp black olives, pitted
     and chopped
2 tbsp chopped fresh flat-leaf
     parsley
1 tbsp chopped fresh oregano
1 cup freshly grated Parmesan
     cheese

method

1 Cut a thin slice off the tops of the tomatoes and discard. Scoop out the seeds with a teaspoon and discard, taking care not to pierce the shells. Turn the tomato shells upside down on paper towels to drain.

2 Heat 6 tablespoons of the olive oil in a skillet, add the onions and garlic, and cook over low heat, stirring occasionally, for 5 minutes, until softened. Remove the skillet from the heat and stir in the breadcrumbs, anchovies, olives, and herbs.

3 Using a teaspoon, fill the tomato shells with the breadcrumb mixture, then place in an ovenproof dish large enough to hold them in a single layer. Sprinkle the tops with grated Parmesan and drizzle with the remaining oil.

4 Bake in a preheated oven, 350°F/180°C, for 20–25 minutes, until the tomatoes are tender and the topping is golden brown.

5 Remove the dish from the oven and serve immediately, if serving hot, or let cool to room temperature.

tuscan bean soup

ingredients

serves 4

¾ cup dried white beans
3½ oz/100 g pancetta
½ small green or savoy cabbage,
    thick stems removed and
    leaves shredded, cut into strips
2 carrots, sliced
14 oz/400 g canned peeled
    tomatoes
4 cups meat stock
1 tbsp chopped fresh oregano
1 onion
4 slices day-old Tuscan
    country bread
½ cup grated Parmesan cheese
2 tbsp olive oil
salt and pepper

method

1 Soak the beans overnight in 4 cups of water. The next
    day, bring to a boil in the soaking water and cook for
    1 hour, until tender.

2 Finely dice the pancetta. Add it to a large pan and
    gently cook until the fat begins to run. Sauté the
    cabbage and carrots in the fat. Mash the tomatoes
    with a fork and add them to the pan. Pour in the stock
    and season with the oregano and salt and pepper.

3 When the beans have cooked, pour off the cooking
    water, add the beans to the soup, and cook for another
    15 minutes. Slice the onion into very thin rings.

4 Toast the bread, cut it in half, and place in four
    ovenproof soup bowls. Pour the soup over the bread
    and top with onion rings. Sprinkle with Parmesan
    and drizzle with the olive oil. Bake in a preheated
    oven, 400°F/200°C, until the onion rings are golden
    brown. Serve.

white bean soup

ingredients

serves 4

1 cup dried cannellini beans,
    soaked overnight in
    cold water
7 cups chicken or vegetable stock
4 oz/115 g dried corallini,
    conchigliette piccole, or other
    soup pasta
⅓ cup olive oil
2 garlic cloves, finely chopped
salt and pepper

method

1 Drain the soaked beans and place them in a large,
   heavy-bottom pan. Add the stock and bring to a boil.
   Partially cover the pan, reduce the heat, and let simmer
   for 2 hours, until tender.

2 Transfer about half the beans and a little of the stock to
   a food processor or blender and process to a smooth
   purée. Return the purée to the pan and stir well to mix.
   Bring the soup back to a boil.

3 Add the pasta to the soup, bring back to a boil and
   cook for 10 minutes, until tender but still firm to
   the bite.

4 Meanwhile, heat ¼ cup of the olive oil in a small
   pan. Add the garlic and cook over low heat, stirring
   frequently, for 4–5 minutes, until golden. Stir the garlic
   into the soup. Season to taste with salt and pepper
   and ladle into warmed soup bowls. Drizzle with the
   remaining olive oil and serve immediately.

fresh tomato soup

ingredients

serves 4

1 tbsp olive oil
1 lb 7 oz/650 g plum tomatoes
1 onion, cut into quarters
1 garlic clove, thinly sliced
1 celery stalk, coarsely chopped
generous 2 cups chicken stock
2 oz/55 g dried anellini or other
   soup pasta
salt and pepper
fresh flat-leaf parsley, chopped,
   to garnish

method

1 Pour the olive oil into a large, heavy-bottom pan and add the tomatoes, onion, garlic, and celery. Cover and cook over low heat for 45 minutes, occasionally shaking the pan gently, until the mixture is pulpy.

2 Transfer the mixture to a food processor or blender and process to a smooth purée. Push the purée through a strainer into a clean pan.

3 Add the stock and bring to a boil. Add the pasta, bring back to a boil, and cook for 8–10 minutes, until the pasta is tender but still firm to the bite. Season to taste with salt and pepper. Ladle into warmed bowls, sprinkle with the parsley, and serve immediately.

minestrone

ingredients

serves 4

3 tbsp olive oil

2 onions, chopped

½ small green or savoy cabbage, thick stems removed, and leaves shredded

2 zucchini, chopped

2 celery stalks, chopped

2 carrots, chopped

2 potatoes, chopped

4 large tomatoes, peeled and chopped

generous ½ cup dried Great Northern beans, soaked overnight in cold water

5 cups chicken or vegetable stock

4 oz/115 g dried soup pasta

salt and pepper

freshly shaved Parmesan cheese, to garnish

freshly grated Parmesan cheese, to serve

method

1 Heat the oil in a large heavy-bottom pan. Add the onions and cook over low heat, stirring occasionally, for 5 minutes, or until softened.

2 Add the cabbage, zucchini, celery, carrots, potatoes, and tomatoes to the pan, cover, and cook, stirring occasionally, for 10 minutes.

3 Drain and rinse the beans, then add to the pan. Pour in the stock, bring to a boil, cover, and simmer for 1–1½ hours, or until the beans are tender.

4 Add the soup pasta to the pan and cook, uncovered, for 8–10 minutes, or until tender but still firm to the bite. Season to taste with salt and pepper and ladle into warmed bowls. Garnish with fresh Parmesan cheese shavings and an extra sprinkling of pepper. Serve the soup, handing around the grated Parmesan cheese separately.

orange salad

ingredients

serves 4

4 oranges
1 red onion
2 tbsp finely chopped parsley
¼ cup olive oil
salt
freshly ground pepper

method

1 Peel the oranges and remove the pith, then slice in rounds. Lay them out in a fan pattern on a plate. Peel and halve the onion, and thinly slice one half. Finely chop the other and combine with the parsley.

2 Sprinkle the sliced and chopped onions over the orange slices, season with a little salt and pepper, and drizzle olive oil over the salad. Cover with plastic wrap and marinate for 1 hour in the refrigerator. Remove from the refrigerator 5 minutes before serving.

pasta salad with charbroiled bell peppers

ingredients

serves 4

1 red bell pepper
1 orange bell pepper
10 oz/280 g dried conchiglie
generous ¼ cup extra virgin
    olive oil
2 tbsp lemon juice
1 garlic clove, chopped
3 tbsp shredded fresh
    basil leaves
salt

pesto

4 tbsp fresh basil leaves
1 tbsp pine nuts
1 garlic clove
generous ¼ cup freshly grated
    Parmesan cheese
3 tbsp extra virgin olive oil

method

1 Put the whole bell peppers on a baking sheet and place under a preheated broiler, turning frequently, for 15 minutes, until charred all over. Remove with tongs and place in a bowl. Cover with crumpled paper towels and set aside.

2 Meanwhile, make the pesto. Put the basil, pine nuts, and garlic into a mortar and pound to a paste with a pestle. Transfer to a bowl and gradually work in the Parmesan with a wooden spoon, followed by the olive oil to make a thick, creamy sauce.

3 Bring a large pan of lightly salted water to a boil. Add the pasta, bring back to a boil, and cook for 8–10 minutes, until tender but still firm to the bite.

4 Combine the olive oil, lemon juice, pesto, and garlic in a bowl, whisking well to mix. Drain the pasta, add it to the pesto mixture while still hot, and toss well. Set aside.

5 When the bell peppers are cool enough to handle, peel off the skins, then cut open and remove the seeds. Slice the flesh coarsely and add to the pasta with the basil. Season to taste with salt and pepper and toss well. Serve at room temperature.

warm pasta salad

ingredients

serves 4

8 oz/225 g dried farfalle or other
  pasta shapes
6 pieces of sun-dried tomato in oil,
  drained and chopped
4 scallions, chopped
2 oz/55 g arugula, shredded
½ cucumber, seeded and diced
2 tbsp freshly grated Parmesan
  cheese
salt and pepper

dressing

¼ cup olive oil
½ tsp superfine sugar
1 tbsp white wine vinegar
1 tsp Dijon mustard
4 fresh basil leaves, finely shredded
salt and pepper

method

1 To make the dressing, whisk the olive oil, sugar, vinegar, and mustard together in a bowl. Season to taste with salt and pepper. Stir in the basil.

2 Bring a large, heavy-bottom pan of lightly salted water to a boil. Add the pasta, return to a boil, and cook for 8–10 minutes, or until tender but still firm to the bite. Drain and transfer to a salad bowl. Add the dressing and toss well.

3 Add the chopped sun-dried tomatoes, scallions, arugula, and cucumber, season to taste with salt and pepper, and toss. Sprinkle with the Parmesan cheese and serve warm.

three-color salad

ingredients

serves 4

10 oz/280 g buffalo mozzarella,
    drained and thinly sliced
8 plum tomatoes, sliced
20 fresh basil leaves
½ cup extra virgin olive oil
salt and pepper

method

1 Arrange the cheese and tomato slices on four individual serving plates and season to taste with salt. Set aside in the refrigerator for 30 minutes.

2 Sprinkle the basil leaves over the salad and drizzle with the olive oil. Season with pepper and serve the salad immediately.

variation

Slice 2 ripe avocado pears and alternate with the mozzarella cheese and tomatoes in the salad.

mozzarella salad
with sun-dried tomatoes

ingredients

serves 4

5 oz/140 g sun-dried tomatoes
   in olive oil (drained weight),
   reserving the oil from
   the bottle
1 tbsp fresh basil, coarsely
   shredded
1 tbsp fresh flat-leaf parsley,
   coarsely chopped
1 tbsp capers, rinsed
1 tbsp balsamic vinegar
1 garlic clove, coarsely chopped
extra olive oil, if necessary
3½ oz/100 g mixed salad greens,
   such as oak leaf lettuce, baby
   spinach, and arugula
1 lb 2 oz/500 g smoked
   mozzarella, sliced
pepper

method

1 Put the sun-dried tomatoes, basil, parsley, capers, vinegar, and garlic in a food processor or blender. Measure the oil from the sun-dried tomatoes jar and add in enough extra oil to make ⅔ cup. Add it to the food processor or blender and process until smooth. Season to taste with pepper.

2 Divide the salad greens between four individual serving plates. Top with the slices of mozzarella and spoon the dressing over them. Serve immediately.

meat & poultry

fillet of beef in laurel wreath

ingredients

serves 4

4 beef tenderloin steaks,
  9 oz/250 g each
4 tsp spicy mustard
12 fresh bay leaves
3 tbsp olive oil
1 tbsp peppercorns,
  coarsely crushed
¼ cup Italian brandy
salt

method

1 Brush the edges of the steaks with the mustard. Place 3 bay leaves around each steak and secure with kitchen twine. Season with salt.

2 Heat the olive oil in an ovenproof pan and thoroughly brown the steaks on both sides, then cook in a preheated oven, 265°F/130°C, for 15–20 minutes.

3 Place the steaks on warmed plates. Pour off the frying fat and sprinkle the peppercorns in the pan. Pour in the brandy, heat slightly, then flambé. Drizzle the brandy sauce over the steaks and serve immediately.

broiled steak with tomatoes & garlic

ingredients

serves 4

3 tbsp olive oil, plus extra
    for brushing
1 lb 9 oz/700 g tomatoes,
    peeled and chopped
1 red bell pepper, seeded
    and chopped
1 onion, chopped
2 garlic cloves, finely chopped
1 tbsp chopped fresh flat-leaf
    parsley
1 tsp dried oregano
1 tsp sugar
4 sirloin steaks, 6 oz/175 g each
salt and pepper

method.

1 To make the sauce, place the oil, tomatoes, red bell pepper, onion, garlic, parsley, oregano, and sugar in a heavy-bottom pan and season to taste with salt and pepper. Bring to a boil, reduce the heat, and let simmer for 15 minutes.

2 Meanwhile, trim any fat around the outsides of the steaks. Season each generously with pepper (but no salt) and brush with olive oil. Cook on a preheated broiler pan according to taste: 2–3 minutes each side for rare; 3–4 minutes each side for medium; 4–5 minutes on each side for well done.

3 Transfer the steaks to warmed individual plates and spoon the sauce over them. Serve immediately.

spaghetti with meatballs

ingredients

serves 6

1 potato, diced
14 oz/400 g ground steak
1 onion, finely chopped
1 egg
3 tbsp chopped fresh flat-leaf
    parsley
all-purpose flour, for dusting
generous ¼ cup virgin olive oil
1¾ cups strained tomatoes
2 tbsp tomato paste
14 oz/400 g dried spaghetti
salt and pepper
freshly grated Parmesan cheese,
    to garnish

method

1 Place the potato in a small pan, add cold water to cover and a pinch of salt, and bring to a boil. Cook for 10–15 minutes, until tender, then drain. Either mash thoroughly with a potato masher or fork or pass through a potato ricer.

2 Combine the potato, steak, onion, egg, and parsley in a bowl and season to taste with salt and pepper. Spread out the flour on a plate. With dampened hands, shape the meat mixture into walnut-size balls and roll in the flour. Shake off any excess.

3 Heat the oil in a heavy-bottom skillet, add the meatballs, and cook over medium heat, stirring and turning frequently, for 8–10 minutes, until golden all over.

4 Add the strained tomatoes and tomato paste and cook for an additional 10 minutes, until the sauce is reduced and thickened.

5 Meanwhile, bring a large pan of lightly salted water to a boil. Add the pasta, bring back to a boil, and cook for 8–10 minutes, until tender but still firm to the bite.

6 Drain well and add to the meatball sauce, tossing well to coat. Transfer to a warmed serving dish, garnish with the basil leaves and Parmesan, and serve immediately.

spaghetti bolognese

ingredients

serves 4

2 tbsp olive oil
1 tbsp butter
1 small onion, finely chopped
1 carrot, finely chopped
1 celery stalk, finely chopped
2/3 cup diced mushrooms
8 oz/225 g ground beef
2¾ oz/75 g unsmoked bacon
    or ham, diced
2 chicken livers, chopped
2 tbsp tomato paste
½ cup dry white wine
½ tsp freshly grated nutmeg
1¼ cups chicken stock
½ cup heavy cream
1 lb/450 g dried spaghetti
salt and pepper
2 tbsp chopped fresh
    flat-leaf parsley, to garnish
freshly grated Parmesan cheese,
    to serve

method

1 Heat the olive oil and butter in a large pan over medium heat. Add the onion, carrot, celery, and mushrooms to the pan, then cook until soft. Add the ground beef and bacon and cook until the beef is evenly browned.

2 Stir in the chicken livers and tomato paste and cook for 2–3 minutes. Pour in the wine and season with salt, pepper, and the nutmeg. Add the stock. Bring to a boil, then cover and simmer gently over low heat for 1 hour. Stir in the cream and simmer, uncovered, until reduced.

3 Bring a large pan of lightly salted water to a boil. Add the pasta, return to a boil, and cook until tender but still firm to the bite. Drain and transfer to a warmed serving dish.

4 Spoon the meat sauce over the pasta, garnish with parsley, and serve with Parmesan cheese.

baked lasagna

ingredients

serves 4

2 tbsp olive oil
2 oz/55 g bacon, chopped
1 garlic clove, chopped
1 onion, chopped
8 oz/225 g ground beef
2 carrots, chopped
2 celery sticks, chopped
2 cups chopped mushrooms
¼ cup red wine
⅔ cup beef stock
1 tbsp sun-dried tomato paste
8 oz/225 g lasagna
1 cup grated Parmesan cheese
salt and pepper
mixed salad, to serve

tomato sauce

2 tbsp olive oil
1 small onion, finely chopped
1 garlic clove, finely chopped
1 bell green pepper, chopped
8 oz/225 g chopped tomatoes
1 tbsp tomato paste
1 tbsp light brown sugar
salt and pepper

method

1 To make the tomato sauce, heat the olive oil in a saucepan. Add the onion, garlic, and bell pepper and cook over a low heat, for 5 minutes, until softened. Add the tomatoes, tomato paste, and sugar, and season to taste with salt and pepper. Cover and let simmer for 30 minutes, until thickened. Set aside to cool until needed.

2 Heat the oil in a large saucepan. Add the bacon and cook over medium heat, stirring occasionally, for 2–3 minutes. Reduce the heat to low, add the garlic and onion and cook for 5 minutes, until softened.

3 Add the ground beef, increase the heat to medium and cook, stirring frequently and breaking it up with a wooden spoon, for 8–10 minutes, until evenly browned. Stir in the carrots, celery, and mushrooms and cook, stirring occasionally, for an additional 5 minutes. Add the wine and stock and stir in the tomato paste. Season to taste with salt and pepper. Bring to a boil, reduce the heat, and simmer for 40 minutes.

4 Make alternating layers of the beef sauce, lasagna and Parmesan in a large, rectangular ovenproof dish. Pour the tomato sauce over the top to cover completely. Bake in a preheated oven, 375°F/190°C, for 30 minutes. Remove from the oven and let stand for 10 minutes. Serve with a mixed salad.

meatball surprise

ingredients

serves 4

1 lb 2 oz/500 g ground steak
1 lb 2 oz/500 g ground pork
2 garlic cloves, finely chopped
1 cup fresh breadcrumbs
scant ½ cup freshly grated
    Parmesan cheese
1 tsp dried oregano
½ tsp ground cinnamon
grated rind and juice
    of 1 lemon
2 eggs, lightly beaten
5½ oz/150 g fontina cheese
⅓ cup virgin olive oil
1¼ cups dried, uncolored
    breadcrumbs
salt and pepper
fresh flat-leaf parsley sprigs,
    to garnish
1 quantity of tomato sauce
    (see page 52), to serve

method

1 Make 1 quantity of tomato sauce and set aside.

2 Combine the steak, pork, garlic, fresh breadcrumbs, Parmesan, oregano, cinnamon, and lemon rind in a bowl. Stir in the lemon juice and beaten eggs, season with salt and pepper, and mix well. Knead the mixture with dampened hands, then shape small quantities into 16 balls.

3 Cut the fontina into 16 cubes and press 1 cube into each meatball, then reshape them to enclose the cheese completely.

4 Heat the olive oil in a large, heavy-bottom skillet. Meanwhile, spread out the dried breadcrumbs on a shallow plate and roll the meatballs in them to coat.

5 Add the meatballs, in batches, to the skillet and cook until golden brown all over. Transfer to an ovenproof dish using a slotted spoon and bake in a preheated oven, 350°F/180°C, for 15–20 minutes, until cooked through. Serve immediately, garnished with parsley sprigs and accompanied with the tomato sauce.

pizzettes

ingredients

serves 6–8

1½ oz/40 g compressed fresh
   yeast, crumbled, or
   2 envelopes active dry yeast
½ tsp sugar
½ cup lukewarm water
3 cups white all-purpose flour,
   plus extra for dusting
1 tsp salt
¼ cup olive oil, plus extra for
   greasing and drizzling
generous ¼ cup water

topping

1 lb 2 oz/500 g tomatoes
1 radicchio
3½ oz/100 g bacon, cut into strips
scant ½ cup pine nuts

method

1 Put the yeast into a small bowl and sprinkle with the sugar. Add the lukewarm water, then stir to dissolve the yeast and sugar. Cover with a clean kitchen towel and leave in a warm spot for 30 minutes. Sift the flour into a large bowl. Make a hollow in the center and pour the yeast mixture, salt, olive oil, and water into it. Knead everything into a smooth, silky dough, then shape it into a ball. Dust the ball with a little flour, cover, and set aside in a warm place to rise for about 1 hour, or until doubled in volume.

2 Grease 2 baking sheets with olive oil. Peel and quarter the tomatoes, remove the seeds, and dice. Trim the radicchio and break it into bite-size pieces.

3 Divide the dough into 12 equal pieces. Form each one into a ball, flatten, and place the rounds on the baking sheets. Top with the diced tomato and bacon and drizzle a little oil. Bake in a preheated oven, 400°F/200°C, for 15 minutes, then sprinkle the radicchio and pine nuts over the pizzette and bake for another 5 minutes. Serve immediately.

stuffed veal cutlets with peperonata

ingredients

serves 4

2 pickled anchovy fillets
1 tbsp capers
1 garlic clove
1 small sprig each of
    rosemary and sage
3 tbsp olive oil
4 veal cutlets, 7 oz/200 g each
salt
1 onion, finely chopped
freshly ground pepper

peperonata

2 each of red, green and yellow
    bell peppers, seeded
1 lb 2 oz/500 g tomatoes
1 tbsp olive oil
2 onions, finely chopped
2 garlic cloves, finely chopped
1 bay leaf
1 dried chile, crumbled
3 tbsp balsamic vinegar
1 pinch sugar
1 small sprig rosemary
salt and pepper

method

1 To make the peperonata, cut the bell peppers into bite-size pieces. Coarsely chop the tomatoes. Heat the olive oil in a large saucepan and sauté the onions. Add the bell peppers and garlic and let simmer for 5 minutes. Add the tomatoes, bay leaf, and chile. Stir in the vinegar and sugar. Cover and let simmer for 15 minutes. Season to taste and add the rosemary. Pour into a pitcher and leave overnight.

2 Rinse and drain the anchovies and capers in a colander. Peel the garlic clove. Strip the rosemary leaves from the branch and pluck the sage leaves. Place these ingredients in a mortar or blender, add pepper and 1 tablespoon of the olive oil, and work into a paste.

3 Wash the meat and pat it dry. Using a sharp knife, cut a pocket horizontally into each cutlet. Stuff the pockets with the anchovy paste and secure with toothpicks. Season with salt and pepper.

4 Heat the remaining olive oil in a pan and brown the cutlets on both sides, then place in a baking dish. Sauté the onion in the pan. Add the peperonata, heat, and spread over the meat. Bake in a preheated oven, 325°F/160°C, for 20 minutes. Serve.

veal with prosciutto & sage

ingredients

serves 4

4 veal scallops
2 tbsp lemon juice
1 tbsp chopped fresh
　　sage leaves
4 slices prosciutto
¼ cup unsalted butter
3 tbsp dry white wine
salt and pepper

method

1 Place the veal scallops between two sheets of plastic wrap and pound with the flat end of a meat mallet or the side of a rolling pin until very thin. Transfer to a plate and sprinkle with the lemon juice. Set aside for 30 minutes, spooning the juice over them occasionally.

2 Pat the scallops dry with paper towels, season with salt and pepper, and rub with half the sage. Place a slice of prosciutto on each scallop and secure with a toothpick.

3 Melt the butter in a large, heavy-bottom skillet. Add the remaining sage and cook over low heat, stirring constantly, for 1 minute. Add the scallops and cook for 3–4 minutes on each side, until golden brown. Pour in the wine and cook for an additional 2 minutes.

4 Transfer the scallops to a warmed serving dish and pour the pan juices over them. Remove and discard the toothpicks and serve immediately.

pappardelle with rabbit sauce

ingredients

serves 4

4 rabbit legs
¼ cup olive oil
1 onion, finely diced
1 carrot, diced
1 celery stalk, diced
generous 1 cup red wine
14 oz/400 g pappardelle
salt and pepper
1 tbsp finely chopped parsley,
    to garnish

method

1 Wash the rabbit legs, pat them dry, and vigorously rub them with salt and pepper.

2 Heat the olive oil in a Dutch oven and sauté the diced vegetables. Add the rabbit legs and brown on both sides. Deglaze with the wine, cover, and cook on low heat for about 40 minutes, until the meat is done. Then take the legs out of the sauce. Remove the meat from the bones, cut it into small cubes, and put the meat back into the sauce.

3 Bring a large pan of lightly salted water to a boil. Add the pasta and cook until tender but still firm to the bite. Mix the drained pasta into the sauce. Add salt and pepper to taste. Serve sprinkled with parsley.

cannelloni with spinach & ricotta

ingredients

serves 4

12 dried cannelloni tubes,
     3 inches/7.5 cm long
butter, for greasing

filling

5 oz/140 g lean ham, chopped
¾ cup frozen spinach, thawed
     and drained
scant ½ cup ricotta cheese
1 egg
3 tbsp freshly grated
     Pecorino Romano cheese
pinch of freshly grated nutmeg
salt and pepper

cheese sauce

2½ cups milk
2 tbsp unsalted butter
2 tbsp all-purpose flour
¾ cup freshly grated Gruyère
     cheese
salt and pepper

method

1 Bring a large pan of lightly salted water to a boil. Add the cannelloni tubes, bring back to a boil, and cook for 6–7 minutes, until nearly tender. Drain and rinse under cold water. Spread out the tubes on a clean dish towel.

2 Put the ham, spinach, and ricotta into a food processor and process until combined. Add the egg and Pecorino and process to a smooth paste. Scrape the filling into a bowl, add the nutmeg and season to taste.

3 Grease an ovenproof dish with butter. Spoon the filling into a piping bag fitted with a ½-inch/1-cm nozzle. Carefully pipe the filling in to the cannelloni tubes and place in the dish.

4 To make the cheese sauce, heat the milk to just below boiling point. Melt the butter in another pan. Stir in the flour and cook over low heat, stirring constantly, for 1 minute. Gradually stir in the hot milk, then bring to a boil, stirring constantly. Let simmer over a low heat, for 10 minutes, until thickened and smooth. Remove from the heat, stir in the Gruyère, and season to taste.

5 Spoon the cheese sauce over the filled cannelloni. Cover the dish with foil and bake in a preheated oven, 350°F/180°C, for 20–25 minutes. Serve immediately.

spaghetti alla carbonara

ingredients

serves 4

1 lb/450 g dried spaghetti
1 tbsp olive oil
8 oz/225 g rindless pancetta
    or lean bacon, chopped
4 eggs
generous ¼ cup light cream
¾ cup freshly grated Parmesan
    cheese
salt and pepper

method

1 Bring a large, heavy-bottom pan of lightly salted water to a boil. Add the pasta, return to a boil, and cook for 8–10 minutes, or until tender but still firm to the bite.

2 Meanwhile, heat the olive oil in a heavy-bottom skillet. Add the chopped pancetta and cook over medium heat, stirring frequently, for 8–10 minutes.

3 Beat the eggs with the cream in a small bowl and season to taste with salt and pepper. Drain the pasta and return it to the pan. Tip in the contents of the skillet, then add the egg mixture and half the Parmesan cheese. Stir well, then transfer to a warmed serving dish. Serve immediately, sprinkled with the remaining Parmesan cheese.

variation

Add ⅓ cup sliced mushrooms to the chopped pancetta and fry together in the olive oil.

sausages with borlotti beans

ingredients

serves 4

2 tbsp virgin olive oil
1 lb 2 oz/500 g luganega
    or other Italian sausages
5 oz/140 g smoked pancetta,
    or lean bacon, diced
2 red onions, chopped
2 garlic cloves, finely chopped
1⅓ cups dried borlotti beans,
    soaked overnight in
    cold water
2 tsp finely chopped
    fresh rosemary
2 tsp chopped fresh sage
1¼ cups dry white wine
salt and pepper
fresh rosemary sprigs,
    to garnish
crusty bread, to serve

method

1 Heat the oil in a Dutch oven. Add the sausages and cook over low heat, turning frequently, for about 10 minutes, until browned all over. Remove from the casserole and set aside.

2 Add the pancetta to the casserole, increase the heat to medium and cook, stirring frequently, for 5 minutes, or until golden brown. Remove with a slotted spoon and set aside.

3 Add the onions to the casserole and cook over low heat, stirring occasionally, for 5 minutes, until softened. Add the garlic and cook for an additional 2 minutes.

4 Drain the beans and set aside the soaking liquid. Add the beans to the casserole, then return the sausages and pancetta. Gently stir in the herbs and pour in the wine. Measure the reserved soaking liquid and add 1¼ cups to the casserole. Season to taste with salt and pepper. Bring to a boil over low heat and boil for 15 minutes, then transfer to a preheated oven, 275°F/140°C, and cook for 2¾ hours.

5 Remove the casserole from the oven and ladle the sausages and beans onto 4 warmed serving plates. Garnish with the rosemary sprigs and serve immediately with crusty bread.

sausage & rosemary risotto

ingredients

serves 4

2 long fresh rosemary sprigs,
    plus extra to garnish
2 tbsp olive oil
¼ cup butter
1 large onion, finely chopped
1 celery stalk, finely chopped
2 garlic cloves, finely chopped
½ tsp dried thyme leaves
1 lb/450 g pork sausage,
    such as luganega or
    cumberland, cut into
    ½-inch/1-cm pieces
generous ½ cup risotto rice
½ cup fruity red wine
generous 5½ cups simmering
    chicken stock
¾ cup freshly grated Parmesan
    cheese
salt and pepper

method

1 Strip the long thin leaves from the rosemary sprigs and chop finely, then set aside.

2 Heat the oil and half the butter in a deep pan over medium heat. Add the onion and celery and cook, stirring occasionally, for 2 minutes. Stir in the garlic, thyme, sausage, and rosemary. Cook, stirring frequently, for 5 minutes, or until the sausage starts to brown. Transfer the sausage to a plate.

3 Reduce the heat and stir in the rice. Cook, stirring constantly, for 2–3 minutes, or until the grains are translucent.

4 Add the wine and cook, stirring constantly, for 1 minute until reduced. Gradually add the hot stock, a ladleful at a time. Stir constantly and add more liquid as the rice absorbs each addition. Increase the heat to medium so that the liquid bubbles. Cook for 20 minutes, or until all the liquid is absorbed and the rice is creamy.

5 Toward the end of cooking, return the sausage pieces to the risotto and heat through. Season to taste with salt and pepper. Remove from the heat and add the remaining butter. Mix well, then stir in the Parmesan until it melts. Spoon the risotto onto warmed plates, garnish with rosemary sprigs, and serve.

spicy pork risotto

ingredients

serves 4

1 thick slice white bread, crust
removed and discarded, soaked
in water or milk for 5 minutes
1 lb/450 g fresh ground pork
2 garlic cloves, minced
1 tbsp finely chopped onion
1 tsp black peppercorns,
lightly crushed
pinch of salt
1 egg
corn oil, for pan-frying
14 oz/400 g canned tomatoes
1 tbsp tomato paste
1 tsp dried oregano
1 tsp fennel seeds
pinch of sugar
3 tbsp butter
1 tbsp olive oil
1 small onion, finely chopped
scant ½ cup risotto rice
⅔ cup red wine
4 cups simmering beef stock
salt and pepper
fresh basil leaves, to garnish

method

1 Drain the bread soaked in milk and squeeze well to
remove all the liquid. Mix the bread, pork, garlic, onion,
crushed peppercorns, and salt together in a bowl. Add
the egg and mix well.

2 Heat some corn oil in a skillet over medium heat. Form
the meat mixture into balls and cook until browned.
Remove each batch from the skillet and drain.

3 Combine the tomatoes, tomato paste, oregano, fennel
seeds, and sugar in a heavy-bottom pan. Add the
meatballs. Bring the sauce to a boil over medium heat,
then reduce the heat and let simmer for 30 minutes.

4 Melt 2 tablespoons of the butter with the olive oil in
a deep pan over medium heat. Stir in the onion and
cook, stirring frequently, for 5 minutes, or until soft.
Reduce the heat, add the rice. Cook, stirring constantly,
for 2–3 minutes, or until the grains are translucent.
Add the wine and cook, stirring constantly, for
1 minute until reduced. Gradually add the hot stock,
stirring constantly until the liquid is absorbed and the
rice is creamy. Season to taste.

5 Lift out the cooked meatballs and add to the risotto.
Remove from the heat and add the remaining butter.
Mix well. Arrange the risotto and meatballs on plates.
Drizzle with tomato sauce, garnish with basil, and serve.

pork with fennel seeds & garlic

ingredients

serves 4

1 lb 5 oz/600 g lean pork
2–3 tbsp olive oil
1 tsp fennel seeds
5 garlic cloves, finely chopped
1 fresh red chile, seeded and
　　finely chopped
10½ oz/300 g tomatoes,
　　peeled and diced
salt and pepper
fresh basil leaves, to garnish

method

1 Wash the meat, pat dry, and cut it into bite-size pieces. Heat the olive oil in a Dutch oven. Add the fennel seeds and garlic to the pot. Season the meat with salt and pepper.

2 Brown the meat on all sides in the hot olive oil. As soon as the meat browns, add the chile and tomatoes. Cover the pot and cook over low heat for about 1 hour, adding a little warm water as needed. Serve the stew immediately, garnished with basil sprigs.

variation

For a traditional Italian addition to the stew, add ⅓ cup canned cannellini beans, drained and rinsed, to the pot 30 minutes before serving.

pepperoni pasta

ingredients

serves 4

3 tbsp olive oil
1 onion, chopped
1 red bell pepper, seeded
 and diced
1 orange bell pepper,
 seeded and diced
1 lb 12 oz/800 g canned
 chopped tomatoes
1 tbsp sun-dried tomato paste
1 tsp paprika
8 oz/225 g pepperoni, sliced
2 tbsp chopped fresh
 flat-leaf parsley, plus extra
 to garnish
1 lb/450 g dried garganelli
salt and pepper
mixed salad greens, to serve

method

1 Heat 2 tablespoons of the olive oil in a large, heavy-bottom skillet. Add the onion and cook over low heat, stirring occasionally, for 5 minutes, or until softened. Add the red and orange bell peppers, tomatoes and their can juices, sun-dried tomato paste, and paprika to the pan and bring to a boil.

2 Add the pepperoni and parsley and season to taste with salt and pepper. Stir well and bring to a boil, then reduce the heat and simmer for 10–15 minutes.

3 Meanwhile, bring a large, heavy-bottom pan of lightly salted water to a boil. Add the pasta, return to a boil, and cook for 8–10 minutes, or until tender but still firm to the bite. Drain well and transfer to a warmed serving dish. Add the remaining olive oil and toss. Add the sauce and toss again. Sprinkle with parsley and serve immediately with mixed salad greens.

roast lamb with rosemary & marsala

ingredients

serves 6

4 lb/1.8 kg leg of lamb
2 garlic cloves, thinly sliced
2 tbsp fresh rosemary leaves
½ cup olive oil
2 lb/900 g potatoes, cut into
    1-inch/2.5-cm cubes
6 fresh sage leaves, chopped
⅔ cup Marsala
salt and pepper

method

1 Use a small, sharp knife to make incisions all over the lamb, opening them out slightly to make little pockets. Insert the garlic slices and about half the rosemary leaves in the pockets.

2 Place the lamb in a roasting pan and spoon over half the olive oil. Roast in a preheated oven, 425°F/220°C, for 15 minutes. Reduce the oven temperature to 350°F/180°C. Remove the lamb from the oven and season to taste with salt and pepper. Turn the lamb over, return to the oven, and roast for an additional 20 minutes.

3 Meanwhile, spread out the cubed potatoes in a second roasting pan, pour the remaining olive oil over them, and toss to coat. Sprinkle with the rosemary and sage. Roast the potatoes and lamb for a further 40 minutes.

4 Remove the lamb from the oven, turn it over, and pour over the Marsala. Return it to the oven with the potatoes and cook for an additional 15 minutes. Remove the lamb to a serving dish and cover with foil. Place the roasting pan over high heat and bring the juices to a boil. Continue to boil until thickened and syrupy. Strain into a warmed pitcher. Carve the lamb into slices and serve with the potatoes and sauce.

lamb shanks with roasted onions

ingredients

serves 4

4 lamb shanks, 12 oz/350 g each,
    with any extra fat trimmed off
6 garlic cloves, each cut into
    slices lengthways
2 tbsp virgin olive oil
1 tbsp very finely chopped
    fresh rosemary
4 red onions
12 oz/350 g carrots, cut
    into thin sticks
¼ cup water
salt and pepper

method

1 Using a small, sharp knife, make incisions in each shank. Insert garlic slices in the incisions of each lamb shank. Place the lamb in a single layer in a roasting pan, drizzle with the olive oil, sprinkle with the rosemary, and season with pepper. Roast in a preheated oven, 350°F/180°C, for 45 minutes.

2 Wrap each onion in a square of foil. Remove the lamb shanks from the oven and season with salt. Return the pan to the oven and place the onions next to it. Roast for an additional 1 hour, or until the lamb is tender.

3 Meanwhile, bring a large pan of water to a boil. Add the carrot sticks and blanch for 1 minute. Drain and refresh under cold water.

4 Remove the roasting pan from the oven when the lamb is meltingly tender and transfer the lamb to a warmed serving dish. Skim off any fat from the roasting pan and place it over medium heat. Add the carrots and cook for 2 minutes, then add the water, bring to a boil, and let simmer, stirring constantly and scraping up the glazed bits from the bottom of the roasting pan.

5 Transfer the carrots and sauce to the serving dish. Remove the onions from the oven and unwrap. Cut and discard about ½ inch/1 cm off the tops of the onions and add them to the dish. Serve immediately.

grilled chicken

ingredients

serves 4

1 corn-fed chicken, about
    2 lb 10 oz / 1.2 kg
2 tsp grated lemon rind
3 garlic cloves, thinly sliced
juice of 3 lemons
⅓ cup olive oil
salt and pepper

method

1 Wash the chicken, pat it dry, and cut in half lengthwise. Lay the chicken halves in a bowl and season them with pepper. Spread the lemon rind and garlic over the chicken. Pour on the lemon juice and olive oil, then cover and marinate overnight in the refrigerator.

2 The next day, take the chicken halves out of the marinade and let drain. Season the meat with salt and grill it slowly on a charcoal or gas grill on medium heat until crisp on both sides and the juices run clear when a skewer is inserted into the thickest part of the meat. Brush the chicken occasionally with the marinade while grilling.

tuscan chicken

ingredients

serves 4

2 tbsp all-purpose flour
4 skinned chicken quarters
   or portions
3 tbsp olive oil
1 red onion, chopped
2 garlic cloves, finely chopped
1 red bell pepper, seeded
   and chopped
pinch of saffron threads
$2/3$ cup chicken stock or a mixture
   of chicken stock and dry
   white wine
14 oz/400 g canned tomatoes,
   chopped
4 sun-dried tomatoes in oil,
   drained and chopped
3 cups sliced portobello
   mushrooms
$2/3$ cup black olives, pitted
2 fl oz/60 ml lemon juice
salt and pepper
fresh basil leaves, to garnish

method

1 Place the flour on a shallow plate and season with salt and pepper. Coat the chicken in the seasoned flour, shaking off any excess. Heat the olive oil in a large, flameproof casserole. Add the chicken and cook over medium heat, turning frequently, for 5–7 minutes, until golden brown. Remove from the casserole and set aside.

2 Add the onion, garlic, and red bell pepper to the casserole, reduce the heat and cook, stirring occasionally, for 5 minutes, until softened. Meanwhile, stir the saffron into the stock.

3 Stir the tomatoes with the juice from the can, the sun-dried tomatoes, mushrooms, and olives into the casserole and cook, stirring occasionally, for 3 minutes. Pour in the stock and saffron mixture and the lemon juice. Bring to a boil, then return the chicken pieces to the casserole.

4 Cover and cook in a preheated oven, 350°F/180°C, for 1 hour, until the chicken is tender. Garnish with the basil leaves and serve immediately.

creamy chicken ravioli

ingredients

serves 4

4 oz/115 g cooked skinless,
   boneless chicken breast,
   coarsely chopped
2 oz/55 g prosciutto,
   coarsely chopped
1 shallot, coarsely chopped
¼ cup ricotta cheese
½ cup freshly grated Pecorino
   Romano cheese
pinch of freshly grated nutmeg
2 eggs, lightly beaten
1 quantity basic pasta dough
   (see page 148, omitting
   spinach from the recipe)
all-purpose flour, for dusting
2 tbsp fresh basil, plus extra to
   garnish

sauce

1¼ cups heavy cream
2 garlic cloves, finely chopped
1¾ cups thinly sliced cremini
   mushrooms
¼ cup freshly grated Pecorino
   Romano cheese
salt and pepper

method

1 Place the chicken, prosciutto, and shallot in a food
   processor and process until chopped and blended.
   Transfer to a bowl, stir in the ricotta cheese,
   2 tablespoons of the grated cheese, the nutmeg, and
   half the egg. Season to taste with salt and pepper.

2 Halve the pasta dough. Wrap one piece in plastic wrap
   and thinly roll out the other on a lightly floured counter.
   Cover with a dish towel and roll out the second piece
   of dough. Place small mounds of the filling in rows
   1½ inches/4 cm apart on one sheet of dough and
   brush the spaces in between with beaten egg. Lift the
   second piece of dough to fit on top. Press down firmly
   between the mounds of filling, pushing out any air.
   Cut into squares and let the ravioli rest for 1 hour.

3 Bring a large pan of lightly salted water to a boil. Add
   the ravioli, in batches, return to a boil, and cook for
   5 minutes. Remove with a slotted spoon and drain
   on paper towels, then transfer to a warmed dish.

4 Meanwhile, to make the sauce, pour the cream into
   a skillet, add the garlic, and bring to a boil. Simmer
   for 1 minute, then add the mushrooms and half of the
   cheese. Season to taste and simmer for 3 minutes. Stir
   in the basil, then pour the sauce over the ravioli. Serve
   sprinkled with any remaining cheese and basil.

chicken tortellini

ingredients

serves 4

4 oz/115 g boneless chicken
    breast, skinned
2 oz/55 g prosciutto
1½ oz/40 g cooked spinach,
    well drained
1 tbsp finely chopped onion
2 tbsp freshly grated
    Parmesan cheese
pinch of ground allspice
1 egg, beaten
1 quantity basic pasta dough
    (see page 148, omitting
    spinach from the recipe)
salt and pepper
2 tbsp chopped fresh parsley,
    to garnish

sauce

1¼ cups light cream
2 garlic cloves, crushed
1¾ cups thinly sliced white
    mushrooms
¼ cup freshly grated
    Parmesan cheese
salt and pepper

method

1 Bring a pan of salted water to a boil. Add the chicken and poach for about 10 minutes. Let cool slightly, then place in a food processor with the prosciutto, spinach, and onion and process until finely chopped. Stir in the Parmesan cheese, allspice, and egg and season with salt and pepper to taste.

2 Thinly roll out the pasta dough and cut into 1½–2-inch/4–5-cm circles.

3 Place ½ teaspoon of the chicken and ham filling in the center of each circle. Fold the pieces in half and press the edges to seal, then wrap each piece round your index finger, cross over the ends, and curl the rest of the dough backward to make a navel shape. Re-roll the trimmings and repeat until all of the dough is used up.

4 Bring a pan of salted water to a boil. Add the tortellini, in batches, return to a boil and cook for 5 minutes. Drain the tortellini well and transfer to a serving dish.

5 To make the sauce, bring the cream and garlic to a boil in a small pan, then simmer for 3 minutes. Add the mushrooms and half of the cheese, season to taste with salt and pepper, and simmer for 2–3 minutes. Pour the sauce over the tortellini. Sprinkle over the remaining Parmesan cheese, garnish with the parsley, and serve.

fish & seafood

sole with artichokes

ingredients

serves 1–2

8 small purple artichokes
juice of 1 lemon
½ cup/125 ml olive oil
4 garlic cloves, finely sliced
1 cup/250 ml dry white wine
1⅔ cup/400 ml stock
1 lb 12 oz/800 g fillet of sole
salt
freshly ground pepper
flour for coating
1 tbsp finely chopped parsley

method

1 Clean the artichokes, shorten the stems to about 1½ inches/4 cm, and peel them. Remove the tough outer leaves and trim the hard thorns from the remaining leaves. Mix the lemon juice and some water in a bowl. Slice the artichokes lengthwise and immediately put them in the lemon water. Marinate for a short time, then pour off the liquid and dab the artichokes dry.

2 Heat 6 tablespoons of the olive oil in a large pan and sauté the artichokes. Add the garlic and sauté until golden brown. Deglaze with the wine, pour in the stock, and add salt and pepper. Simmer for 20–25 minutes, then remove from the stovetop.

3 Season the fish fillets with salt and pepper, coat in flour, and shake off the excess. Heat the remaining oil and fry the fish on both sides. Serve the fish over the artichokes, sprinkled with the chopped parsley.

white fish stew

ingredients

serves 4

2¼ lb/1 kg white fish, cleaned, and gutted
2 tbsp olive oil
1 onion, chopped finely
2 garlic cloves, finely chopped
2 carrots, diced
2 celery stalks, diced
9 oz/250 g tomatoes, peeled and quartered, diced
2¼ cups fish stock
2 bay leaves
1 tbsp balsamic vinegar
4 slices white bread
salt and pepper

method

1 Wash the fish, pat it dry, and cut into bite-size pieces. Season with salt and pepper.

2 Heat the olive oil in a deep pan and sauté the onion and garlic. Add the carrots and celery, browning lightly. Mix in the tomatoes, pour in the fish stock, and add the bay leaves. Simmer together for 10 minutes.

3 Add the fish to the stew and cook on low heat for about 10 minutes. Remove the bay leaves and season the stew with salt, pepper, and the balsamic vinegar. Toast the white bread and place each slice in a deep bowl. Ladle the fish stew over the toast and serve immediately.

fried anchovies

ingredients

serves 4

1 lb/500 g anchovies (or sardines),
　as small as possible
flour, for coating
2 tbsp olive oil
coarse sea salt
1 lemon, to serve

method.

1 Wash the anchovies. If the fish are larger than
3½ inches/9 cm, cut off and discard the heads. If
they are smaller, you can use the entire fish. Coat
the anchovies with flour and tap off the excess.

2 Heat the olive oil in a skillet, add the fish, and cook
for a minute or so, turning them over to cook on both
sides. Place the anchovies on a plate and sprinkle with
coarse sea salt. Cut the lemon into quarters and serve
with the anchovies.

seafood-stuffed artichokes

ingredients

serves 4

4 large, globe artichokes
1¼ cups water
3 tbsp lemon juice
¼ cup olive oil
1 small onion, finely chopped
2 garlic cloves, finely chopped
9 oz/250 g frozen, precooked
    mixed seafood
2 tbsp finely chopped parsley
2 tbsp breadcrumbs
salt and pepper

method

1 Remove the stems and leaves from the artichokes. Carefully remove the fuzzy choke from the inside with a spoon and wash the artichoke bottoms.

2 Combine the water with the lemon juice, and a little salt in a pan and bring to a boil. Add the artichoke bottoms and cook for 30 minutes, then set them upside down in a sieve to drain.

3 Heat 2 tablespoons of the olive oil in a pan and sauté the onion and garlic. Add the frozen seafood and cook until the thawing liquid evaporates. Then remove from the stove, stir in the parsley, and season with salt and pepper. Stuff the artichoke bottoms with the seafood mixture. Preheat the oven broiler.

4 Place the stuffed artichokes side by side in a baking dish, sprinkle with the breadcrumbs, and drizzle with the remaining olive oil. Cook under a preheated broiler until golden brown. Serve immediately.

trout fillets with mushrooms

ingredients

serves 4

8 trout fillets, gutted
  and boned
1 tbsp chopped fresh tarragon
2¼ cups white wine
generous 1 lb 2 oz/500 g
  porcini mushrooms
scant 4 tbsp butter
1 small onion, finely chopped
1 tbsp chopped fresh thyme
salt and pepper

method

1 Wash the trout fillets, pat them dry, and rub with salt and pepper. Place the fish in a bowl, sprinkle with the tarragon, and pour ½ cup of wine over them. Cover the bowl and marinate for 30 minutes.

2 Meanwhile, wipe the porcini mushrooms with a damp cloth, trim the stems, and cut into ¾-inch/1-cm thick slices. Heat half of the butter in a large, heavy-bottom skillet and sauté the onion until translucent. Add the mushrooms and sauté, stirring, until all the liquid has evaporated. Pour in the rest of the wine and season with salt, pepper, and the thyme. Simmer on a low heat for 10 minutes.

3 Melt the rest of the butter in a large, nonstick skillet. Remove the trout fillets from the marinade, pat them dry, and sauté in hot butter for 3 minutes on each side. Then pour in the marinade and bring it to a boil. Serve the mushrooms with the fish.

red mullet with capers & olives

ingredients

serves 4

1 lb 9 oz/700 g red snapper fillets
(about 12)
3 tbsp chopped fresh marjoram
or flat-leaf parsley
thinly peeled rind of 1 orange,
cut into thin strips
8 oz/225 g mixed salad greens,
torn into pieces
3 tbsp virgin olive oil
1 fennel bulb, cut into thin sticks
salt and pepper

dressing

3 tbsp extra virgin olive oil
1 tbsp balsamic vinegar
1 tbsp white wine vinegar
1 tsp Dijon mustard
salt and pepper

sauce

1 tbsp butter
¼ cup black olives, pitted
and thinly sliced
1 tbsp capers, rinsed

method

1 Place the fish fillets on a large plate, sprinkle with the marjoram, and season with salt and pepper. Set aside.

2 Blanch the orange rind in a small pan of boiling water for 2 minutes, drain, refresh under cold water, and drain well again. Place the salad greens in a large bowl.

3 To make the dressing, whisk together the extra virgin olive oil, vinegars, and mustard in a small bowl and season to taste. Pour the dressing over the salad greens and toss well. Arrange the salad leaves on a large serving platter to make a bed.

4 Heat the virgin olive oil in a large, heavy-bottom skillet. Add the fennel and cook, stirring constantly, for 1 minute. Remove the fennel with a slotted spoon, set aside, and keep warm. Add the fish fillets, skin-side down, and cook for 2 minutes. Carefully turn them over and cook for an additional 1–2 minutes. Remove from the skillet and drain on paper towels. Keep warm.

5 To make the sauce, melt the butter in a small pan, add the olives and capers, and cook, stirring constantly, for 1 minute.

6 Place the fish fillets on the bed of salad greens, top with the orange rind and fennel, and pour over the sauce. Serve immediately.

swordfish with olives & capers

ingredients

serves 4

2 tbsp all-purpose flour
4 swordfish steaks, 8 oz/225 g
    each
generous ⅓ cup olive oil
2 garlic cloves, halved
1 onion, chopped
4 anchovy fillets, drained
    and chopped
4 tomatoes, peeled, seeded,
    and chopped
12 green olives, pitted and sliced
1 tbsp capers, rinsed
salt and pepper
fresh rosemary leaves,
    to garnish

method

1 Spread out the flour on a plate and season with salt and pepper. Coat the fish in the seasoned flour, shaking off any excess.

2 Gently heat the olive oil in a large, heavy-bottom skillet. Add the garlic and cook over low heat for 2–3 minutes, until just golden. Do not let it turn brown or burn. Remove the garlic and discard.

3 Add the fish to the skillet and cook over medium heat for about 4 minutes on each side, until cooked through and golden brown. Remove the steaks from the skillet and set aside.

4 Add the onion and anchovies to the skillet and cook, mashing the anchovies with a wooden spoon until they have turned to a purée and the onion is golden. Add the tomatoes and cook over low heat, stirring occasionally, for about 20 minutes, until the mixture has thickened.

5 Stir in the olives and capers and taste and adjust the seasoning. Return the steaks to the skillet and heat through gently. Serve garnished with rosemary.

grilled sardines with lemon sauce

ingredients

serves 4

1 large lemon
5 tbsp unsalted butter
20 fresh sardines, cleaned
   and heads removed
1 tbsp chopped fresh fennel
   leaves
salt and pepper

method

1 Peel the lemon. Remove all the bitter pith and discard. Using a small, serrated knife, cut between the membranes and ease out the flesh segments, discarding any seeds. Chop finely and set aside.

2 Melt 2 tablespoons of the butter in a small pan and season with salt and pepper. Brush the sardines all over with the melted butter and cook under a preheated broiler or on a barbecue, turning once, for 5–6 minutes, until cooked through.

3 Meanwhile, melt the remaining butter, then remove the pan from the heat. Stir in the chopped lemon and fennel.

4 Transfer the sardines to a warmed platter, pour the sauce over them, and serve immediately.

linguine with anchovies, olives & capers

ingredients

serves 4

3 tbsp olive oil
2 garlic cloves, finely chopped
10 anchovy fillets, drained
　　and chopped
scant 1 cup black olives, pitted
　　and chopped
1 tbsp capers, rinsed
1 lb/450 g plum tomatoes,
　　peeled, seeded, and chopped
pinch of cayenne pepper
salt
14 oz/400 g dried linguine
2 tbsp chopped fresh flat-leaf
　　parsley, to garnish

method

1 Heat the olive oil in a heavy-bottom pan. Add the garlic and cook over low heat, stirring frequently, for 2 minutes. Add the anchovies and mash them to a pulp with a fork. Add the olives, capers, and tomatoes and season to taste with cayenne pepper. Cover and let simmer for 25 minutes.

2 Meanwhile, bring a pan of lightly salted water to a boil. Add the pasta, bring back to a boil, and cook for 8–10 minutes, until tender but still firm to the bite. Drain and transfer to a warmed serving dish.

3 Spoon the anchovy sauce into the dish and toss the pasta, using two large forks. Garnish with the parsley and serve immediately.

sicilian tuna

ingredients

serves 4

4 tuna steaks, 5 oz/140 g each
2 fennel bulbs, sliced
    thickly lengthwise
2 red onions, sliced
2 tbsp virgin olive oil
crusty rolls, to serve

marinade

½ cup extra virgin olive oil
4 garlic cloves, finely chopped
4 fresh red chiles, seeded and
    finely chopped
juice and finely grated rind
    of 2 lemons
3 tbsp finely chopped fresh
    flat-leaf parsley
salt and pepper

method

1 First, make the marinade by whisking all the ingredients together in a bowl. Place the tuna steaks in a large shallow dish and spoon over 3 tablespoons of the marinade, turning to coat. Cover and set aside for 30 minutes. Set aside the remaining marinade.

2 Heat a ridged broiler pan. Put the fennel and onions in a bowl, add the oil, and toss well to coat. Add to the broiler pan and cook for 5 minutes on each side, until just starting to color. Transfer to four warmed serving plates, drizzle with the reserved marinade, and keep warm.

3 Add the tuna steaks to the broiler pan and cook, turning once, for 4–5 minutes, until firm to the touch but still moist inside. Transfer the tuna to the plates and serve immediately with crusty rolls.

beans with tuna

ingredients

serves 4

1 lb 12 oz/800 g Great Northern
    beans, soaked overnight in
    cold water
⅓ cup extra virgin olive oil
2 tuna steaks, 7 oz/200 g each
2 garlic cloves, lightly crushed
sprig of fresh sage
2 tbsp water
salt and pepper
4 chopped fresh sage leaves,
    to garnish

method

1 Drain the soaked beans and place them in a pan. Add
enough water to cover and bring to a boil and boil
for 10 minutes. Reduce the heat and let simmer for
1–1½ hours, until tender. Drain the beans thoroughly.

2 Heat 1 tablespoon of the olive oil in a heavy-bottom
skillet. Add the tuna steaks and cook over medium
heat for 3–4 minutes on each side, until tender.
Remove from the skillet and set aside to cool.

3 Heat 3 tablespoons of the remaining olive oil in a
heavy-bottom skillet. Add the garlic and sage sprig
and cook briefly over low heat until the sage starts to
sizzle. Remove the garlic and discard.

4 Add the beans and cook for 1 minute, then add the
water and season to taste with salt and pepper. Cook
until the water has been absorbed. Remove and
discard the sage sprig, transfer the beans to a bowl,
and set aside to cool.

5 Meanwhile, flake the tuna, removing any bones. When
the beans are lukewarm or at room temperature,
according to taste, gently stir in the tuna. Drizzle with
the remaining olive oil, sprinkle with the chopped sage,
and serve.

seafood omelet

ingredients

serves 3

2 tbsp unsalted butter
1 tbsp olive oil
1 onion, very finely chopped
6 oz/175 g zucchini, halved
    lengthwise and sliced
1 celery stalk, very finely chopped
1¼ cups mushrooms, sliced
¾ cup green beans, cut into
    2-inch/5-cm lengths
4 eggs
scant ½ cup mascarpone cheese
1 tbsp chopped fresh thyme
1 tbsp shredded fresh basil
7 oz/200 g canned tuna,
    drained and flaked
4 oz/115 g cooked, peeled shrimp
salt and pepper

method

1 Melt the butter with the olive oil in a heavy-bottom skillet with a flameproof handle. If the skillet has a wooden handle, protect it with foil because it needs to go under the broiler. Add the onion and cook over low heat, stirring occasionally, for 5 minutes, until softened.

2 Add the zucchini, celery, mushrooms, and beans and cook, stirring occasionally, for an additional 8–10 minutes, until starting to brown.

3 Beat the eggs with the mascarpone, thyme, basil, and salt and pepper to taste.

4 Add the tuna to the skillet and stir it into the mixture with a wooden spoon. Add the shrimp.

5 Pour the egg mixture into the skillet and cook for 5 minutes, until it is just starting to set. Draw the egg from the sides of the skillet toward the center to let the uncooked egg run underneath.

6 Put the skillet under a preheated broiler and cook until the egg is just set and the surface is starting to brown. Cut the omelet into wedges and serve.

tuna with garlic, lemon, capers & olives

ingredients

serves 4

3 cups dried gnocchi

¼ cup olive oil

¼ cup butter

3 large garlic cloves, thinly sliced

7 oz/200 g canned tuna, drained and broken into chunks

2 tbsp lemon juice

1 tbsp capers, drained

10–12 black olives, pitted and sliced

2 tbsp chopped fresh flat-leaf parsley, to serve

method

1 Cook the gnocchi following the instructions on the packet until al dente. Drain and return to the pan.

2 Heat the olive oil and half the butter in a skillet over a medium–low heat. Add the garlic and cook for a few seconds, or until just beginning to color. Reduce the heat to low. Add the tuna, lemon juice, capers, and olives. Stir the mixture gently until all the ingredients are heated through.

3 Transfer the gnocchi to a warm serving dish. Pour the tuna mixture over the pasta. Add the parsley and remaining butter. Toss the gnocchi well to mix and serve immediately.

risotto with tuna & pine nuts

ingredients

serves 4

5 tbsp butter
¼ cup olive oil
1 small onion, finely chopped
scant 1½ cups risotto rice
5 cups simmering fish or
    chicken stock
8 oz/225 g tuna, canned and
    drained, or broiled fresh
    steaks
8–10 black olives, pitted and sliced
1 small pimiento, thinly sliced
1 tsp finely chopped fresh parsley
1 tsp finely chopped
    fresh marjoram
2 tbsp white wine vinegar
scant ½ cup pine nuts
1 garlic clove, chopped
8 oz/225 g fresh tomatoes,
    peeled, seeded, and diced
¾ cup Parmesan or Grana Padano
    cheese
salt and pepper

method

1 Melt 2 tablespoons of the butter with 1 tablespoon of the oil in a deep pan over medium heat. Add the onion and cook, stirring, for 5 minutes, or until soft and starting to turn golden. Reduce the heat, add the rice, and mix to coat in the butter and oil. Cook, stirring constantly, for 2–3 minutes, or until the grains are translucent. Add the stock, a ladleful at a time, stirring constantly, until all the liquid is absorbed and the rice is creamy. Season to taste.

2 While the risotto is cooking, flake the tuna into a bowl and mix in the olives, pimiento, parsley, marjoram, and vinegar. Season to taste with salt and pepper.

3 Heat the remaining oil in a small skillet over high heat. Add the pine nuts and garlic. Cook, stirring constantly, for 2 minutes, or until they just start to brown. Add the tomatoes to the skillet and mix well. Continue cooking over medium heat for 3–4 minutes or until they are thoroughly warm. Pour the tomato mixture over the tuna mixture and mix. Fold into the risotto 5 minutes before the end of the cooking time.

4 Remove the risotto from the heat when all the liquid has been absorbed and add the remaining butter. Mix well, then stir in the Parmesan until it melts. Serve the risotto immediately.

bavettine with smoked salmon & arugula

ingredients

serves 4

12 oz/350 g dried bavettine
    or linguine
2 tbsp olive oil
1 garlic clove, finely chopped
4 oz/115 g smoked salmon,
    cut into thin strips
2 oz/55 g arugula
salt and pepper
½ lemon, to garnish

method

1 Bring a large, heavy-bottom pan of lightly salted water to a boil. Add the pasta, return to a boil, and cook for 8–10 minutes, or until tender but still firm to the bite.

2 Just before the end of the cooking time, heat the olive oil in a heavy-bottom skillet. Add the garlic and cook over low heat, stirring constantly, for 1 minute. Do not allow the garlic to brown or it will taste bitter. Add the salmon and arugula. Season to taste with salt and pepper and cook, stirring constantly, for 1 minute. Remove the skillet from the heat.

3 Drain the pasta and transfer to a warmed serving dish. Add the smoked salmon and arugula mixture, toss lightly, and serve, garnished with a lemon half.

layered spaghetti with smoked salmon & shrimp

ingredients

serves 6

12 oz/350 g dried spaghetti
generous 1 cup butter, plus extra
    for greasing
7 oz/200 g smoked salmon,
    cut into strips
10 oz/280 g large jumbo shrimp,
    cooked, peeled, and deveined
1 cup freshly grated Parmesan
    cheese
salt

béchamel sauce

2 tbsp butter
1 tbsp all-purpose flour
1½ cups warm milk
salt and pepper

method

1 To make the béchamel sauce, melt the butter in a pan on the lowest heat. Add the flour and stir with a wooden spoon. Turn up the heat and continue cooking for 2 minutes, stirring all the time. Add half of the milk and stir to make a smooth paste. Add the remaining milk, stirring until you have a smooth, white sauce. Season with salt and pepper.

2 Bring a large pan of lightly salted water to a boil. Add the pasta, bring back to a boil, and cook for 8–10 minutes, until tender but still firm to the bite. Drain well, return to the pan, add 4 tablespoons of the butter, and toss well.

3 Butter a large, ovenproof dish and set aside. Spoon half the spaghetti into the prepared dish, cover with the strips of smoked salmon, then top with the shrimp. Pour over half the béchamel sauce and sprinkle with half the Parmesan. Add the remaining spaghetti, cover with the remaining sauce, and sprinkle with the remaining Parmesan. Dice the remaining butter and dot it over the surface.

4 Bake in a preheated oven, 350°F/180°C, for 15 minutes, until the top is golden. Serve immediately.

springtime pasta

ingredients

serves 4

2 tbsp lemon juice
4 baby globe artichokes
½ cup olive oil
2 shallots, finely chopped
2 garlic cloves, finely chopped
2 tbsp chopped fresh
    flat-leaf parsley
2 tbsp chopped fresh mint
12 oz/350 g dried rigatoni or
    other tubular pasta
12 large uncooked shrimp
2 tbsp unsalted butter
salt and pepper

method

1 Fill a bowl with cold water and add the lemon juice. Prepare the artichokes one at a time. Cut off the stems and trim away any tough outer leaves. Cut across the tops of the leaves. Slice in half lengthwise and remove the central fibrous chokes, then cut lengthwise into ¼-inch/5-mm thick slices. Place the slices in the bowl of acidulated water to prevent discoloration.

2 Heat ⅓ cup of the olive oil in a heavy-bottom skillet. Drain the artichoke slices and pat dry with paper towels. Add them to the skillet with the shallots, garlic, parsley, and mint, and cook over low heat, stirring frequently, for 10–12 minutes until tender.

3 Meanwhile, bring a large pan of lightly salted water to a boil. Add the pasta, bring back to a boil, and cook for 8–10 minutes, until tender but still firm to the bite.

4 Peel the shrimp, cut a slit along the back of each, and remove and discard the dark vein. Melt the butter in a small skillet, cut the shrimp in half, and add them to the skillet. Cook, stirring occasionally, for 2–3 minutes, until they have changed color. Season to taste.

5 Drain the pasta and pour it into a bowl. Add the remaining olive oil and toss well. Add the artichoke mixture and the shrimp and toss again. Serve the pasta immediately.

scallops with porcini & cream sauce

ingredients

serves 4

1⅓ cups dried porcini mushrooms
generous 2 cups hot water
3 tbsp olive oil
2½ cups butter
1½ cups sliced scallops
2 garlic cloves, very finely
    chopped
2 tbsp lemon juice
generous 1 cup heavy cream
12 oz/350 g dried fettuccine
    or pappardelle
salt and pepper
2 tbsp chopped fresh
    flat-leaf parsley, to serve

method

1 Put the porcini and hot water in a bowl. Let soak for 20 minutes. Strain the mushrooms, reserving the soaking water, and chop coarsely. Line a strainer with paper towels and strain the mushroom water into a bowl.

2 Heat the oil and butter in a large skillet over a medium heat. Add the scallops and cook for 2 minutes, or until just golden. Add the garlic and mushrooms, then stir-fry for another minute.

3 Stir in the lemon juice, cream, and ⅔ cup of the mushroom water. Bring to a boil, then simmer over a medium heat for 2–3 minutes, stirring constantly, until the liquid is reduced by half. Season with salt and pepper. Remove from the heat.

4 Meanwhile, bring a large pan of lightly salted water to the boil. Add the pasta, bring back to the boil and cook for 8–10 minutes, until tender but firm. Briefly reheat the sauce and pour over the pasta. Sprinkle with the parsley and toss well to mix. Serve immediately.

saffron & lemon risotto with scallops

ingredients

serves 4

16 scallops, shucked
juice of 1 lemon, plus extra
    for seasoning
1 tbsp olive oil, plus extra
    for brushing
2½ cups butter
1 small onion, finely chopped
scant 1½ cups risotto rice
5 cups simmering fish or
    vegetable stock
1 tsp crumbled saffron threads
2 tbsp vegetable oil
1 cup freshly grated Parmesan
    or Grana Padano cheese
salt and pepper
1 lemon, cut into wedges
2 tsp grated lemon zest,
    to garnish

method

1 Place the scallops in a nonmetallic bowl and mix with the lemon juice. Cover the bowl with plastic wrap and let chill in the refrigerator for 15 minutes.

2 Heat the olive oil with 2 tablespoons of the butter in a deep pan over medium heat until the butter has melted. Add the onion and cook, stirring, for 5 minutes, or until soft. Add the rice and mix to coat in oil and butter. Cook, stirring constantly, for 2–3 minutes, or until the grains are translucent. Dissolve the saffron in ¼ cup of hot stock and add to the rice. Add the remaining stock, stirring constantly, until all the liquid is absorbed and the rice is creamy. Season with salt and pepper.

3 When the risotto is nearly cooked, preheat a broiler pan over high heat. Brush the scallops with oil and cook for 3–4 minutes on each side. Take care not to overcook or they will be rubbery.

4 Remove the risotto from the heat and add the remaining butter. Mix well, then stir in the Parmesan until it melts. Season with lemon juice, adding just 1 teaspoon at a time and tasting as you go. Serve the risotto immediately with the scallops and lemon wedges arranged on top, sprinkled with lemon zest.

seafood pizza

ingredients

serves 2

all-purpose flour, for dusting
virgin olive oil, for drizzling
1 quantity tomato sauce
    (see page 52)
8 oz/225 g mixed fresh seafood
½ red bell pepper, seeded and
    chopped
½ yellow bell pepper, seeded
    and chopped
1 tbsp capers, rinsed
1 cup Taleggio cheese, grated
3 tbsp freshly grated
    Parmesan cheese
½ tsp dried oregano
2¾ oz/75 g anchovy fillets in oil,
    drained and sliced
10 black olives, pitted
salt and pepper

pizza dough

1½ cups white all-purpose flour,
    plus extra for dusting
1 tsp salt
1 tsp active dry yeast
1 tbsp olive oil
⅓ cup lukewarm water

method

1 To make the pizza dough, sift the flour and salt into a bowl and stir in the yeast. Make a well in the center and pour in the oil and water. Incorporate the dry ingredients into the liquid, using floured hands.

2 Turn out the dough onto a lightly floured counter and knead well for 5 minutes, until smooth and elastic. Return to the clean bowl, cover with lightly oiled plastic wrap, and set aside to rise in a warm place for about 1 hour, or until doubled in size.

3 Turn out the dough again onto a lightly floured counter and knock down. Knead briefly, then roll out the dough into a circle about ¼ inch/5 mm thick. Transfer to a lightly oiled baking sheet and push up the edge with your fingers to form a small rim.

4 Spread the tomato sauce over the pizza base, almost to the edge. Arrange the mixed seafood, red and yellow bell peppers, and capers evenly on top.

5 Sprinkle the cheeses and oregano evenly over the topping. Add the anchovy fillets and olives, drizzle with olive oil. Season to taste with salt and pepper.

6 Bake in a preheated oven, 425°F/220°C, for 20–25 minutes, until the crust is crisp and the cheese has melted. Serve immediately.

vegetable dishes

sweet and sour pumpkin

ingredients

serves 4

½ cup olive oil

1 lb 10 oz/750 g pumpkin flesh, cut into pieces

1 garlic clove, finely chopped

1 cinnamon stick

2 cloves

1 tbsp brown sugar

generous ¾ cup mild white wine vinegar

10 basil leaves

salt and pepper

method

1 Heat the olive oil in a deep pan. Add the pumpkin and garlic and sauté. Season with salt and pepper, then add the cinnamon stick and cloves. Cook on a low heat, stirring occasionally, for 30 minutes; the pumpkin should still be firm to the bite.

2 When the pumpkin has cooked, remove the cinnamon and cloves from the pan. Season to taste with the sugar and vinegar. Cut the basil into fine strips and stir in. Serve the pumpkin hot or cold.

spinach in gorgonzola sauce

ingredients

serves 4

2¼ lb/1 kg leaf spinach
¼ cup butter
freshly grated nutmeg
½ cup milk
½ cup white wine
4½ oz/125 g mild Gorgonzola
2 egg yolks
salt and pepper

method

1 Thoroughly wash the spinach, removing any wilted leaves and coarse stems.

2 Melt half the butter in a large pan. Add the spinach while it is still dripping wet and let it wilt. Season with salt, pepper, and nutmeg and keep warm on a low heat.

3 In a saucepan, simmer the milk and wine to reduce slightly. Crumble the Gorgonzola into the saucepan and let it melt, stirring constantly. Remove from the stove. Whisk the egg yolks with a little of the sauce, then add it to the rest of sauce and fold in the spinach. Adjust the seasoning with salt and pepper and serve.

spicy fava beans

ingredients

serves 2

2 tbsp olive oil

4 shallots, finely sliced

2 garlic cloves, finely chopped

2 fresh chiles, halved and chopped

1 cup vegetable stock

2⅓ cups fresh fava beans, shelled

2 sprigs savory

1 bay leaf

2 tomatoes, peeled, seeded, and diced

3½ oz/100 g pancetta, finely diced

1 tbsp finely chopped fresh parsley

salt and pepper

method

1 Heat the olive oil in a pan and fry the shallots, garlic, and chiles. Pour in the vegetable stock and bring to a boil. Add the beans, savory, and bay leaf, cover the pan, and simmer for about 30 minutes.

2 Remove the herbs, stir in the tomatoes, and season to taste with salt and pepper.

3 In an ungreased skillet, fry the pancetta until it is crisp. Stir the pancetta and parsley into the vegetables and serve immediately.

rosemary potatoes

ingredients

serves 4

1 lb 10 oz/750 g waxy potatoes, peeled, and cut into cubes
3 garlic cloves, coarsely chopped
3 sprigs rosemary, chopped
generous ¼ cup olive oil, plus extra for greasing
salt and pepper

method

1 Grease a flat baking dish with olive oil. Place a layer of potatoes on the bottom of the baking dish. Season with some of the garlic and rosemary, salt, and pepper. Repeat this procedure until all the ingredients have been used. Drizzle the olive oil over the top.

2 Bake in a preheated oven, 400°F/200°C, for about 45 minutes, tossing the potatoes several times. Serve in the baking dish while hot.

eggplants with mozzarella & parmesan

ingredients

serves 6–8

3 eggplants, thinly sliced
olive oil, for brushing
10½ oz/300 g buffalo mozzarella, sliced
1 cup freshly grated Parmesan cheese
3 tbsp dried, uncolored breadcrumbs
1 tbsp butter
sprigs of fresh flat-leaf parsley, to garnish

tomato and basil sauce

2 tbsp virgin olive oil
4 shallots, finely chopped
2 garlic cloves, finely chopped
14 oz/400 g canned tomatoes
1 tsp sugar
8 fresh basil leaves, shredded
salt and pepper

method

1 Arrange the eggplant slices in a single layer on one or two lightly oiled large cookie sheets. Brush with olive oil and bake in a preheated oven, 400°F/200°C, for 15–20 minutes, until tender but not collapsing.

2 Meanwhile, make the tomato and basil sauce. Heat the oil in a heavy-bottom pan, add the shallots and cook, stirring occasionally, for 5 minutes, until softened. Add the garlic and cook for 1 minute more. Add the tomatoes and break them up with a wooden spoon. Stir in the sugar, and season to taste with salt and pepper. Bring to a boil, reduce the heat, and let simmer for about 10 minutes, until thickened. Stir in the basil leaves.

3 Brush an ovenproof dish with olive oil and arrange half the eggplant slices in the bottom. Cover with half the mozzarella, spoon over half the tomato sauce, and sprinkle with half the Parmesan. Mix the remaining Parmesan with the breadcrumbs. Make more layers, ending with the Parmesan mixture.

4 Dot the top with butter and bake for 25 minutes, until the topping is golden brown. Remove from the oven and let stand for 5 minutes, before serving, garnished with the parsley.

baked eggplant & tomatoes

ingredients

serves 4

1 lb 5 oz/600 g eggplant,
    cut into ¹/₂-inch/1-cm
    thick slices
salt
1 lb 5 oz/600 g plum tomatoes,
    cut into ¹/₂-inch/1-cm
    thick slices
1 cup olive oil
¹/₂ cup freshly grated Parmesan
    cheese
2 tbsp fresh white breadcrumbs
pepper

method

1 To remove any bitterness, layer the eggplant slices in a colander, sprinkling each layer with salt. Stand the colander in the sink and let drain for 30 minutes. Meanwhile, spread out the tomato slices on paper towels, cover with more paper towels, and let drain. Rinse the eggplant under cold running water to remove all traces of the salt, then pat dry with paper towels.

2 Heat 2 tablespoons of the olive oil in a large, heavy-bottom skillet. Add the tomato slices and cook for just 30 seconds on each side. Transfer to a large platter and season to taste with salt and pepper.

3 Wipe out the skillet with paper towels, then add 2 tablespoons of the remaining olive oil and heat. Add the eggplant slices, in batches, and cook on both sides until golden brown. Remove from the skillet and drain on paper towels. Cook the remaining slices in the same way, adding more olive oil as required.

4 Brush a large ovenproof dish with some of the remaining olive oil. Arrange alternate layers of eggplant and tomatoes, sprinkling each layer with Parmesan cheese. Top with the breadcrumbs and drizzle with the remaining olive oil.

5 Bake in a preheated oven, 350°F/180°C, for 25–30 minutes, until golden. Serve immediately.

spinach & ricotta dumplings

ingredients

serves 4

2 lb 4 oz/1 kg fresh spinach, coarse stalks removed
1½ cups ricotta cheese
1 cup freshly grated Parmesan cheese
3 eggs, lightly beaten
pinch of freshly grated nutmeg
generous ¾ cup all-purpose flour, plus extra for dusting
salt and pepper

herb butter

½ cup unsalted butter
2 tbsp chopped fresh oregano
2 tbsp chopped fresh sage

method

1 Wash the spinach, then place it in a pan with just the water clinging to its leaves. Cover and cook over low heat for 6–8 minutes, until just wilted. Drain well and set aside to cool.

2 Squeeze or press out as much liquid as possible from the spinach, then chop finely. Place the spinach in a bowl and add the ricotta, half the Parmesan, the eggs, and nutmeg, and season to taste. Beat until thoroughly combined. Sift most of the flour into the mixture and lightly work it in, to make a workable mixture. Cover with plastic wrap and let chill for 1 hour.

3 With floured hands, break off small pieces of the mixture and roll them into walnut-size balls. Handle them as little as possible, because they are quite delicate. Lightly dust the dumplings with flour.

4 Bring a large pan of lightly salted water to a boil. Add the dumplings and cook for 2–3 minutes, until they rise to the surface. Remove them from the pan with a slotted spoon, drain well, and set aside.

5 To make the herb butter, melt the butter in a large, heavy-bottom skillet. Add the oregano and sage and cook over low heat, stirring frequently, for 1 minute. Add the dumplings and toss gently for 1 minute to coat. Serve sprinkled with the remaining Parmesan.

spinach & ricotta ravioli

ingredients

serves 4

12 oz/350 g fresh spinach leaves, washed, and coarse stalks removed
1 cup ricotta cheese
1/2 cup freshly grated Parmesan cheese
2 eggs, lightly beaten
pinch of freshly grated nutmeg
salt and pepper
freshly grated Parmesan cheese, to serve

spinach pasta dough

11/3 cups white all-purpose flour, plus extra for dusting
pinch of salt
8 oz/225 g frozen spinach, thawed, squeezed dry, and finely chopped
2 eggs, lightly beaten
1 tbsp olive oil

method

1 To make the pasta dough, sift the flour into a food processor and add the salt. Add the chopped spinach, then pour in the eggs and olive oil and process until the dough begins to come together. Turn out onto a lightly floured counter and knead until smooth. Wrap in plastic wrap and let rest for at least 30 minutes.

2 Cook the spinach over a low heat for 5 minutes until wilted. Drain and squeeze out as much moisture as possible. Cool, then chop finely. Beat the ricotta cheese until smooth, then stir in the spinach, Parmesan, and half the egg. Season to taste with nutmeg and pepper.

3 Halve the pasta dough. Cover one piece and thinly roll out the other on a floured counter. Cover and roll out the second piece. Put small mounds of filling in rows 1 1/2 inches/4 cm apart on one sheet of dough and brush the spaces in between with the remaining beaten egg. Lay the second piece of dough to fit on top. Press down between the mounds, pushing out any air. Cut into squares and rest on a dish towel for 1 hour.

4 Bring a large pan of salted water to a boil, add the ravioli, in batches, return to a boil, and cook for 5 minutes. Remove with a slotted spoon and drain on paper towels. Serve with grated Parmesan cheese.

vegetarian lasagna

ingredients

serves 4

olive oil, for brushing
2 eggplants, sliced
2 tbsp butter
1 garlic clove, finely chopped
4 zucchini, sliced
1 tbsp finely chopped fresh
    flat-leaf parsley
1 tbsp finely chopped fresh
    marjoram
1 cup mozzarella cheese, grated
2½ cups strained canned tomatoes
175 g/6 oz dried no-precook
    lasagna
salt and pepper
2½ cups béchamel sauce (see
    page 122)
½ cup freshly grated Parmesan
    cheese

method

1 Brush a large ovenproof dish with olive oil. Brush a large broiler pan with olive oil and heat until smoking. Add half the eggplant slices and cook over medium heat for 8 minutes, or until golden brown all over. Remove the eggplant from the broiler pan and drain on paper towels. Add the remaining eggplant slices and extra oil, if necessary, and cook for 8 minutes, or until golden brown all over.

2 Melt the butter in a skillet and add the garlic, zucchini, parsley, and marjoram. Cook over medium heat, stirring frequently, for 5 minutes, or until the zucchini are golden brown all over. Remove from the skillet and let drain on paper towels.

3 Layer the eggplant, zucchini, mozzarella, strained tomatoes, and lasagna in the dish, seasoning with salt and pepper as you go and finishing with a layer of lasagna. Pour over the béchamel sauce, making sure that all the pasta is covered. Sprinkle with the grated Parmesan cheese and bake in the preheated oven, 400°F/200°C, for 30–40 minutes, or until golden brown. Serve the lasagna immediately.

mixed vegetable agnolotti

ingredients

serves 4

butter, for greasing
1 quantity basic pasta dough (see
    page 148, omitting the spinach
    from the recipe)
all-purpose flour, for dusting
3/4 cup freshly grated Parmesan
    cheese
mixed salad greens, to serve

filling

1/2 cup olive oil
1 red onion, chopped
3 garlic cloves, chopped
2 large eggplants, cut into chunks
3 large zucchini, cut into chunks
6 beefsteak tomatoes, peeled,
    seeded, and coarsely chopped
1 large green bell pepper, seeded
    and diced
1 large red bell pepper, seeded
    and diced
1 tbsp sun-dried tomato paste
1 tbsp shredded fresh basil
salt and pepper

method

1 To make the filling, heat the olive oil in a large, heavy-bottom pan. Add the onion and garlic and cook over low heat, stirring occasionally, for 5 minutes, or until softened. Add the eggplant, zucchini, tomatoes, green and red bell peppers, sun-dried tomato paste, and basil. Season to taste with salt and pepper, cover, and let simmer gently, stirring occasionally, for 20 minutes.

2 Lightly grease an ovenproof dish with butter. Roll out the pasta dough on a lightly floured counter and stamp out 3-inch/7.5-cm circles with a plain cutter. Place a spoonful of the vegetable filling on one side of each circle. Dampen the edges slightly and fold the pasta circles over, pressing together to seal.

3 Bring a large pan of lightly salted water to a boil. Add the agnolotti, in batches if necessary, return to a boil, and cook for 3–4 minutes. Remove with a slotted spoon, drain, and transfer to the dish. Sprinkle with the Parmesan cheese and bake in a preheated oven, 400°F/200°C, for 20 minutes. Serve with salad greens.

penne in a creamy mushroom sauce

ingredients

serves 4

¼ cup butter
1 tbsp olive oil
6 shallots, sliced
6 cups cremini mushrooms, sliced
1 tsp all-purpose flour
⅔ cup heavy cream or panna
   da cucina
2 tbsp port
4 oz/115 g sun-dried tomatoes
   in oil, drained and chopped
pinch of freshly grated nutmeg
12 oz/350 g dried penne
salt and pepper
2 tbsp chopped fresh flat-leaf
   parsley, to garnish

method

1 Melt the butter with the olive oil in a large heavy-bottom skillet. Add the shallots and cook over low heat, stirring occasionally, for 4–5 minutes, or until softened. Add the mushrooms and cook over low heat for an additional 2 minutes. Season to taste with salt and pepper, sprinkle in the flour and cook, stirring, for 1 minute.

2 Remove the skillet from the heat and gradually stir in the cream and port. Return to the heat, add the sun-dried tomatoes, and grated nutmeg, and cook over low heat, stirring occasionally, for 8 minutes.

3 Meanwhile, bring a large heavy-bottom pan of lightly salted water to a boil. Add the pasta, return to a boil, and cook for 8–10 minutes, or until tender but still firm to the bite. Drain the pasta well and add to the mushroom sauce. Cook for 3 minutes, then transfer to a warmed serving dish. Sprinkle with the chopped parsley and serve immediately.

baked pasta with mushrooms

ingredients

serves 4

2 quantities of béchamel sauce
(see page 122)
5 oz/140 g fontina cheese,
thinly sliced
5 tbsp butter, plus extra
for greasing
4½ cups mixed exotic mushrooms,
sliced
12 oz/350 g dried tagliatelle
2 egg yolks
scant 1⅓ cups freshly grated
Pecorino Romano cheese
salt and pepper
mixed salad greens, to serve

method

1 Make a double quantity of béchamel sauce. Stir the fontina cheese into the béchamel sauce and set aside.

2 Melt 2 tablespoons of the butter in a large pan. Add the mushrooms and cook over low heat, stirring occasionally, for 10 minutes.

3 Meanwhile, bring a large pan of lightly salted water to a boil. Add the pasta, bring back to a boil, and cook for 8–10 minutes, until tender but still firm to the bite. Drain, return to the pan, and add the remaining butter, the egg yolks, and about one-third of the béchamel sauce, then season to taste with salt and pepper. Toss well to mix, then gently stir in the mushrooms.

4 Lightly grease a large, ovenproof dish and spoon in the pasta mixture. Pour over the remaining sauce evenly and sprinkle with the grated Pecorino. Bake in a preheated oven, 400°F/200°C, for 15–20 minutes, until golden brown. Serve immediately with mixed salad greens.

mushroom cannelloni

ingredients

serves 4

12 dried cannelloni tubes
2 tbsp butter
6 cups mixed wild mushrooms,
    finely chopped
1 garlic clove, finely chopped
1½ cups fresh breadcrumbs
⅔ cup milk
¼ cup olive oil, plus extra
    for brushing
1 cup ricotta cheese
1 cup freshly grated
    Parmesan cheese
2 tbsp pine nuts
2 tbsp slivered almonds
salt and pepper

tomato olive sauce

2 tbsp olive oil
1 onion, finely chopped
1 garlic clove, finely chopped
1 lb 12 oz/800 g canned
    chopped tomatoes
1 tbsp tomato paste
8 pitted black olives, chopped
salt and pepper

method

1 Bring a large pan of lightly salted water to a boil. Add the cannelloni tubes, return to a boil, and cook for 8–10 minutes, or until tender but still firm to the bite. With a slotted spoon, transfer the cannelloni tubes to a plate and pat dry. Brush a large ovenproof dish with olive oil.

2 Meanwhile, make the tomato sauce. Heat the olive oil in a skillet. Add the onion and garlic and cook over low heat for 5 minutes, or until softened. Add the tomatoes and their can juices, tomato paste, and olives and season to taste with salt and pepper. Bring to a boil and cook for 3–4 minutes. Pour the sauce into the ovenproof dish.

3 To make the filling, melt the butter in a heavy-bottom skillet. Add the mushrooms and garlic and cook over medium heat, stirring frequently until tender. Remove the skillet from the heat. Mix the breadcrumbs, milk, and olive oil together in a bowl, then stir in the ricotta, mushroom mixture, and a generous ¾ cup of the Parmesan cheese. Season to taste with salt and pepper.

4 Fill the cannelloni tubes with the mushroom mixture and place them in the dish. Brush with olive oil and sprinkle with the remaining Parmesan cheese, pine nuts, and almonds. Bake in a preheated oven, 375°F/190°C, for 25 minutes, or until golden.

spaghetti with roasted garlic & pepper sauce

ingredients

serves 4

6 large garlic cloves, unpeeled
14 oz/400 g bottled roasted
    red bell peppers, drained
    and sliced
7 oz/200 g canned chopped
    tomatoes
3 tbsp olive oil
¼ tsp dried chile flakes
1 tsp chopped fresh oregano
    or thyme
12 oz/350 g dried spaghetti,
    bucatini, or linguine
salt and pepper
freshly grated Parmesan, to serve

method

1 Place the unpeeled garlic cloves in a shallow, ovenproof dish. Roast in a preheated oven, 400°F/200°C, for 7–10 minutes, or until the cloves feel soft.

2 Put the bell peppers, tomatoes, and oil in a food processor or blender, then purée. Squeeze the garlic flesh into the purée. Add the chile flakes and oregano. Season with salt and pepper. Blend again, then scrape into a pan and set aside.

3 Bring a large heavy-bottom pan of lightly salted water to the boil. Add the pasta, return to the boil and cook for 8–10 minutes, or until tender but still firm to the bite. Drain and transfer to a warm serving dish.

4 Reheat the sauce and pour over the pasta. Toss well to mix. Serve at once with Parmesan.

asparagus & sun-dried tomato risotto

ingredients

serves 4

1 tbsp olive oil
2½ tbsp butter
1 small onion, finely chopped
6 sun-dried tomatoes, thinly sliced
scant 1½ cups risotto rice
⅔ cup dry white wine
4 cups simmering vegetable stock
8 oz/225 g fresh asparagus
    spears, cooked
¾ cup freshly grated Parmesan
    or Grana Padano cheese
salt and pepper
thinly pared lemon rind,
    to garnish

method

1 Heat the olive oil with 2 tablespoons of the butter in a deep pan over medium heat until the butter has melted. Stir in the onion and sun-dried tomatoes, and cook, stirring occasionally, for 5 minutes until the onion is soft and starting to turn golden. Do not brown.

2 Reduce the heat, add the rice, and mix to coat in the oil and butter. Cook, stirring constantly, for 2–3 minutes, or until the grains are translucent. Add the wine and cook, stirring constantly, until it has reduced.

3 Gradually add the hot stock, a ladleful at a time. Stir constantly, until all the liquid is absorbed and the rice is creamy. Season to taste with salt and pepper.

4 While the risotto is cooking, cut most of the asparagus into pieces about 1 inch/2.5 cm long. Keep several spears whole for garnishing the finished dish. Carefully fold the cut pieces of asparagus into the risotto for the last 5 minutes of cooking time.

5 Remove the risotto from the heat and add the remaining butter. Mix well, then stir in the Parmesan until it melts. Spoon the risotto onto individual warmed serving dishes and garnish with whole spears of asparagus. Sprinkle the lemon rind on top and serve.

risotto primavera

ingredients

serves 6–8

8 oz/225 g fresh thin asparagus
    spears
1/4 cup olive oil
2 1/2 cups young green beans, cut
    into 1-inch/2.5-cm lengths
2 1/2 cups young zucchini, quartered
    and cut into 1-inch/2.5-cm
    lengths
generous 1 1/2 cups shelled
    fresh peas
1 onion, finely chopped
1–2 garlic cloves, finely chopped
generous 1 1/2 cups risotto rice
generous 6 1/3 cups simmering
    chicken or vegetable stock
4 scallions, cut into 1-inch/2.5-cm
    lengths
1/4 cup butter
1 cup freshly grated Parmesan
    cheese
2 tbsp snipped fresh chives
2 tbsp shredded fresh basil
salt and pepper

method

1 Trim the woody ends of the asparagus and cut off the tips. Cut the stems into 1-inch/2.5-cm pieces and set aside with the tips.

2 Heat 2 tablespoons of the oil in a large skillet over high heat until very hot. Add the asparagus, beans, zucchini, and peas and stir-fry for 3–4 minutes until they are bright green and just starting to soften. Set aside.

3 Heat the remaining oil in a large, heavy-bottom pan over medium heat. Add the onion and cook, stirring occasionally, for 3 minutes, or until it starts to soften. Stir in the garlic and cook, while stirring, for 30 seconds.

4 Reduce the heat, add the rice, and mix to coat in oil. Cook, stirring constantly, for 2–3 minutes, or until the grains are translucent. Gradually add the hot stock, a ladleful at a time, until all but 2 tablespoons of the liquid is absorbed and the rice is creamy.

5 Stir in the stir-fried vegetables, onion mixture, and scallions with the remaining stock. Cook for 2 minutes, stirring frequently, then season to taste with salt and pepper. Stir in the butter, Parmesan, chives, and basil.

6 Remove the pan from the heat. Transfer the risotto to a warmed serving dish, and serve immediately.

wild mushroom risotto

ingredients

serves 6

½ cup dried porcini or morel
    mushrooms
about 1 lb 2 oz/500 g mixed
    fresh wild mushrooms,
    such as porcini, horse
    mushrooms, and chanterelles,
    halved if large
¼ cup olive oil
3–4 garlic cloves, finely chopped
¼ cup butter
1 onion, finely chopped
generous 1½ cups risotto rice
¼ cup dry white vermouth
5 cups simmering chicken or
    vegetable stock
1 cup freshly grated Parmesan
    cheese
3 tbsp chopped fresh
    flat-leaf parsley
salt and pepper

method

1 Place the dried mushrooms in a heatproof bowl and add boiling water to cover. Soak for 30 minutes, then carefully lift out and pat dry. Strain the liquid through a strainer lined with paper towels and set aside.

2 Trim the fresh mushrooms and gently brush clean. Heat 3 tablespoons of the oil in a large skillet. Add the fresh mushrooms and stir-fry for 1–2 minutes. Add the garlic and the soaked mushrooms and cook, stirring frequently, for 2 minutes. Transfer to a plate.

3 Heat the remaining oil and half the butter in a large, heavy-bottom pan. Add the onion and cook over medium heat, stirring occasionally, for 2 minutes, until softened. Reduce the heat, add the rice and cook, stirring constantly, for 2–3 minutes, or until the grains are translucent. Add the vermouth and cook, stirring constantly, for 1 minute until reduced.

4 Gradually add the hot stock, a ladleful at a time, until all the liquid is absorbed and the rice is creamy. Add half the reserved mushroom soaking liquid to the risotto and stir in the mushrooms. Season to taste and add more mushroom liquid, if necessary.

5 Remove the pan from the heat and stir in the remaining butter, the grated Parmesan, and chopped parsley. Serve immediately.

risotto with four cheeses

ingredients

serves 6

2½ oz unsalted butter
1 red onion, finely chopped
generous 1½ cups risotto rice
scant 1 cup dry white wine
4 cups simmering vegetable stock
½ cup crumbled Gorgonzola cheese
½ cup freshly grated Taleggio
    cheese
½ cup freshly grated fontina cheese
½ cup freshly grated Parmesan
    cheese
salt and pepper
2 tbsp chopped fresh flat-leaf
    parsley, to garnish

method

1 Melt the butter in a large, heavy-bottom pan. Add the onion and cook over low heat, stirring occasionally, for 5 minutes, until softened. Add the rice and cook, stirring constantly, for 2–3 minutes, until all the grains are thoroughly coated and glistening.

2 Add the wine and cook, stirring constantly, until it has almost completely evaporated. Add a ladleful of the hot stock and cook, stirring constantly, until all the stock has been absorbed. Continue cooking, stirring and adding the stock, a ladleful at a time, for about 20 minutes, or until the rice is tender and the liquid has been absorbed.

3 Remove the pan from the heat and stir in the Gorgonzola, Taleggio, fontina, and about one-quarter of the Parmesan until melted. Season to taste with salt and pepper. Transfer the risotto to a warmed serving dish, sprinkle with the remaining Parmesan, garnish with the parsley, and serve immediately.

cheese & tomato pizza

ingredients

serves 4

1 quantity pizza dough
  (see page 130)
6 tomatoes, thinly sliced
6 oz/175 g mozzarella cheese,
  drained and thinly sliced
2 tbsp shredded fresh basil leaves
2 tbsp olive oil
salt and pepper

method

1 To make the base, make 1 quantity of pizza dough. Turn out the dough onto a lightly floured counter and knock down. Knead briefly, then cut it in half and roll out each piece into a circle about ¼ inch/5 mm thick. Transfer to a lightly oiled baking sheet and push up the edges with your fingers to form a small rim.

2 For the topping, arrange the tomato and mozzarella slices alternately over the pizza bases. Season to taste with salt and pepper, sprinkle with the basil, and drizzle with the olive oil.

3 Bake in a preheated oven, 450°F/230°C, for 15–20 minutes, until the crust is crisp and the cheese has melted. Serve immediately.

desserts

tiramisù

ingredients

serves 8

3 eggs
¾ cup golden superfine sugar
⅔ cup self-rising flour
1 tbsp unsweetened cocoa,
    plus extra to decorate
⅔ cup cold black coffee
2 tbsp rum
butter, for greasing

filling

generous 1½ cups mascarpone
    cheese
1 cup fresh custard
¼ cup golden superfine sugar
3½ oz/100 g semisweet
    chocolate, grated

method

1 To make the cake, grease an 8-inch/20-cm round cake pan with butter and line with parchment paper. Place the eggs and sugar in a large bowl and beat together until thick and light. Sift the flour and unsweetened cocoa over the batter and fold in gently. Spoon the batter into the prepared pan and bake in a preheated oven, 350°F/180°C, for 30 minutes, or until the cake springs back when pressed gently in the center. Let stand in the tin for 5 minutes, then turn out onto a wire rack to cool.

2 Place the black coffee and rum in a bowl or cup, mix together and set aside. To make the filling, place the mascarpone cheese in a large bowl and beat until soft. Stir in the custard, then gradually add the sugar, beating constantly. Stir in the grated chocolate.

3 Cut the cake horizontally into three layers and place one layer on a serving plate. Sprinkle with one-third of the coffee mixture, then cover with one-third of the mascarpone mixture. Repeat the layers, finishing with a topping of the mascarpone mixture. Let chill in the refrigerator for 3 hours. Sift over the unsweetened cocoa before serving.

zabaglione

ingredients

serves 2

4 egg yolks
1/3 cup superfine sugar
5 tbsp Marsala
amaretti cookies, to serve

method

1 Whisk the egg yolks with the sugar in a heatproof bowl or, if you have one, the top of a double boiler for about 1 minute.

2 Gently whisk in the Marsala. Set the bowl over a pan of barely simmering water or put the top of the double boiler on its bottom filled with barely simmering water, and whisk vigorously for 10–15 minutes, until thick, creamy and foamy.

3 Immediately pour into serving glasses and serve with amaretti cookies.

lemon granita

ingredients

serves 4

2 cups water
generous ½ cup white
    granulated sugar
1 cup lemon juice
grated rind of 1 lemon
lemon slices, to serve

method.

1 Heat the water in a heavy-bottom pan over low heat. Add the sugar and stir until it has completely dissolved. Bring to a boil, remove the pan from the heat, and set the syrup aside to cool.

2 Stir the lemon juice and rind into the syrup. Pour the mixture into a freezerproof container and place in the freezer for 3–4 hours.

3 To serve, remove the container from the freezer and dip the base into hot water. Turn out the ice block and chop coarsely, then place in a food processor and process until it forms small crystals (granita means "granular"). Spoon into glasses and serve immediately.

apples in white wine

ingredients

serves 4

2 lb 4 oz/1 kg apples
5 tbsp lemon juice
generous 1 cup white wine
1 cup sugar
1 cinnamon stick
2 cloves

method

1 Peel, quarter, and core the apples. Cut them into narrow wedges and immediately sprinkle with the lemon juice.

2 Combine the wine, sugar, cinnamon stick, and cloves in a saucepan and slowly bring to a boil. Add the apples and simmer on low heat for 10 minutes. Remove the apples with a slotted spoon and set them aside.

3 Bring the wine to a boil again and reduce to a thick syrup. Remove the cinnamon stick and cloves. Return the apple wedges to the pan and let them cool in the sauce.

cherry pie

ingredients

serves 4

3¼ cups all-purpose flour
⅔ cup superfine sugar
1 pinch salt
2 eggs
grated rind of 1 orange
⅓ cup cold butter
⅓ cup lard
oil for greasing
14 oz/400 g sour cherry jam
1 egg yolk, whisked
2 tbsp confectioners' sugar

method

1 Sift the flour onto a work surface, mix in the sugar, and make a well in the center. Add the salt, eggs, orange rind, butter, and lard and knead everything into a smooth, supple dough. Form the dough into a ball, cover it in plastic wrap, and chill for at least 1 hour in the refrigerator.

2 Grease a 28-cm/11-inch springform pan. On a floured surface, roll out two-thirds of the dough very thinly and line the bottom and sides of the pan with it. Spread the jam evenly over the dough.

3 Roll out the remaining dough and use a pastry wheel to cut it into strips about ¾ inch/2 cm wide. Use the strips to form a lattice over the jam. Brush the top of the pie with the whisked egg yolk, then bake in a preheated oven, 350°F/180°C, for about 45 minutes.

4 Let the pie cool briefly in the pan, then transfer it to a wire rack. Before serving, dust with confectioners' sugar.

lemon pie

ingredients

serves 8

1½ cups all-purpose flour
generous 1 cup sugar
5 egg yolks
grated rind and juice of 2 lemons
1 pinch salt
scant 4 tbsp chilled butter,
    cut into pieces, plus extra
    for greasing
3 eggs
⅔ cup heavy cream
2 tbsp confectioners' sugar
oil, for greasing

method

1 Sift the flour onto a work surface, then blend in 7 tablespoons of sugar, and make a well in the center. Add 4 egg yolks, half the lemon rind, the salt, and the butter. Knead everything into a smooth, supple dough. Form the dough into a ball, cover it in plastic wrap, and chill for 1 hour in the refrigerator.

2 Lightly grease a 10½-inch/26-cm springform pan. On a floured surface, roll out the dough very thinly and line the bottom and sides of the pan with it. Use a fork to prick several holes in the dough, then lay a sheet of parchment paper over it. Fill the crust with dried beans and bake in a preheated oven, 350°F/180°C, for 15 minutes. Remove the dried beans and parchment paper and let cool.

3 Reduce the oven temperature to 325°F/160°C. Beat the remaining egg yolk, the whole eggs, and the rest of the sugar and lemon rind into a thick, pale cream. Stir in the lemon juice. Whip the cream and fold it into the egg mixture. Spread it evenly in the crust, then bake for 20 minutes. Dust the surface with confectioners' sugar, then return to the oven until golden brown.

venetian donuts

ingredients

serves 6

2 eggs
3 tbsp sugar
2 tsp vanilla sugar
1 pinch salt
1½ cups all-purpose flour
¼ cup olive oil
2 tbsp brandy
1 tsp grated lemon rind
oil, for deep-frying
confectioners' sugar, for dusting

method

1 Beat the eggs with the sugar, vanilla sugar, and salt until foamy. Gradually stir in the flour, olive oil, brandy, and lemon peel. Let the dough rest for 30 minutes, then beat it vigorously, adding a little water or flour, as needed.

2 Heat the oil to 350°F/180°C in a deep pan or a deep-fryer. Use two teaspoons to scoop little balls of dough and drop them in the hot oil. Fry until golden brown. Place on paper towels to drain, and dust with confectioners' sugar before serving.

chocolate & amaretto cheesecake

ingredients

serves 10–12

oil, for brushing
6 oz/175 g graham crackers
2 oz/55 g amaretti cookies
5 tbsp butter

filling

8 oz/225 g semisweet chocolate,
    broken into pieces
1¾ cups cream cheese
generous ½ cup golden superfine
    sugar
3 tbsp all-purpose flour
1 tsp vanilla extract
4 eggs
1¼ cups heavy cream
¼ cup amaretto liqueur

topping

1 tbsp amaretto liqueur
¾ cup sour cream
crushed amaretti cookies

method

1 Line the bottom of a 9-inch/23-cm springform cake pan with foil and brush the sides with oil. Place the crackers and cookies in a plastic bag and crush with a rolling pin. Place the butter in a pan and heat until just melted, then stir in the crushed cookies. Press them into the bottom of the pan and let chill for 1 hour.

2 To make the filling, melt the chocolate in a small heatproof bowl over a saucepan of gently simmering water, then let cool. Place the cream cheese in a bowl and beat until fluffy, then add the sugar, flour, and vanilla extract and beat together until smooth. Gradually add the eggs, beating until well blended. Blend in the melted chocolate, cream, and amaretto liqueur. Pour the mixture over the chilled biscuit base and bake in a preheated oven, 325°F/160°C, for 50–60 minutes, or until set.

3 Leave the cheesecake in the oven with the door slightly ajar, until cold. Run a knife round the inside of the pan to loosen the cheesecake. Let chill in the refrigerator for 2 hours, then remove from the pan and place on a serving plate. To make the topping, stir the amaretto liqueur into the sour cream and spread over the cheesecake. Sprinkle the crushed amaretti cookies round the edge to decorate.

ricotta cheesecake

ingredients

serves 6–8

1⅛ cups all-purpose flour,
   plus extra for dusting
3 tbsp superfine sugar
salt
½ cup unsalted butter,
   chilled and diced
1 egg yolk

filling

2 cups ricotta cheese
½ cup heavy cream
2 eggs, plus 1 egg yolk
scant ½ cup superfine sugar
finely grated rind of 1 lemon
finely grated rind of 1 orange

method

1 To make the pastry, sift the flour with the sugar and a pinch of salt onto a counter and make a well in the center. Add the diced butter and egg yolk to the well and, using your fingertips, gradually work in the flour mixture until fully incorporated. Knead very lightly.

2 Cut off about one-quarter, wrap in plastic wrap, and let chill in the refrigerator. Press the remaining dough into the base of a 9-inch/23-cm tart pan with removable sides. Let chill for 30 minutes.

3 To make the filling, beat the ricotta with the cream, eggs, extra egg yolk, sugar, lemon rind, and orange rind. Cover with plastic wrap and keep cool until required.

4 Prick the base of the pastry shell all over with a fork. Line with foil, fill with dried beans, and bake blind in a preheated oven, 375°F/190°C, for 15 minutes. Remove from the oven and take out the foil and beans. Stand the pan on a wire rack and set aside to cool.

5 Spoon the ricotta mixture into the pastry shell and level the surface. Roll out the reserved pastry, cut it into strips and arrange over the filling in a lattice pattern. Bake in the oven, for 30–35 minutes, until the top of the cheesecake is golden and the filling has set. Let cool on a wire rack before lifting off the side of the pan. Cut into wedges to serve.

almond cake

ingredients

serves 12

3 eggs, separated
generous ½ cup superfine sugar
generous ½ cup potato flour
1 cup almonds, blanched, peeled,
    and finely chopped
finely grated rind of 1 orange
generous ½ cup orange juice
salt
butter, for greasing
confectioners' sugar, for dusting

method

1 Generously grease a round 8-inch/20-cm cake pan with removable sides. Beat the egg yolks with the sugar in a medium bowl until pale and thick and the mixture leaves a ribbon trail when the whisk is lifted. Stir in the potato flour, almonds, orange rind, and orange juice.

2 Whisk the egg whites with a pinch of salt in another bowl until stiff. Gently fold the whites into the egg yolk mixture.

3 Pour the mixture into the pan and bake in a preheated oven, 325°F/160°C, for 50–60 minutes, until golden and just firm to the touch. Turn out onto a wire rack to cool. Sift over a little confectioners' sugar to decorate before serving.

tuscan christmas cake

ingredients

serves 12–14

generous ¾ cup hazelnuts
generous ¾ cup almonds
½ cup finely chopped candied peel
⅓ cup finely chopped dried
    apricots
⅓ cup finely chopped candied
    pineapple
grated rind of 1 orange
scant ½ cup all-purpose flour
2 tbsp unsweetened cocoa
1 tsp ground cinnamon
¼ tsp ground coriander
¼ tsp freshly grated nutmeg
¼ tsp ground cloves
generous ½ cup superfine sugar
½ cup honey
confectioners' sugar, to decorate

method

1 Line an 8-inch/20-cm cake pan with removable sides with parchment paper. Spread out the hazelnuts on a baking sheet and toast in a preheated oven, 350°F/180°C, for 10 minutes, until golden brown. Pour them onto a dish towel and rub off the skins.

2 Meanwhile, spread out the almonds on a baking sheet and toast in the oven for 10 minutes, until golden. Reduce the oven temperature to 300°F/150°C. Chop all the nuts and place in a large bowl.

3 Add the candied peel, apricots, pineapple, and orange rind to the nuts and mix well. Sift together the flour, unsweetened cocoa, cinnamon, coriander, nutmeg, and cloves into the bowl and mix well.

4 Put the sugar and honey into a pan and set over low heat, stirring, until the sugar has dissolved. Bring to a boil and cook for 5 minutes, until thickened. Stir the nut mixture into the pan and remove from the heat.

5 Spoon the mixture into the prepared cake pan and level the surface. Bake in the oven for 1 hour, then transfer to a wire rack to cool in the pan.

6 Remove the cake from the pan and peel off the parchment paper. Just before serving, dredge the top with confectioners' sugar. Cut into thin wedges to serve.

chestnut & chocolate terrine

ingredients

serves 6

generous ¾ cup heavy cream
4 oz/115 g semisweet
    chocolate, melted and cooled
generous ⅓ cup rum
1 package rectangular, plain,
    sweet cookies
8 oz/225 g canned sweetened
    chestnut purée
unsweetened cocoa, for dusting
confectioners' sugar,
    to decorate

method

1 Line a 1-lb/450-g loaf pan with plastic wrap. Place the cream in a bowl and whip lightly until soft peaks form. Using a spatula, fold in the cooled chocolate.

2 Place the rum in a shallow dish. Lightly dip 4 cookies into the rum and arrange on the bottom of the pan. Repeat with 4 more cookies. Spread half the chocolate cream over the cookies. Make another layer of 8 cookies dipped in rum and spread over the chestnut purée, followed by another layer of cookies. Spread over the remaining chocolate cream and top with a final layer of cookies. Cover with plastic wrap and let chill for 8 hours, or preferably overnight.

3 Turn the terrine out onto a large serving dish. Dust with unsweetened cocoa. Cut strips of paper and place these randomly on top of the terrine. Sift over confectioners' sugar. Carefully remove the paper. To serve, dip a sharp knife in hot water, dry it, and use it to cut the terrine into slices.

italian chocolate christmas pudding

ingredients

serves 10

½ cup mixed candied fruit, chopped

⅓ cup raisins

grated rind of ½ orange

3 tbsp orange juice

3 tbsp light cream

12 oz/350 g semisweet chocolate, chopped

½ cup cream cheese

4 oz/115 g amaretti cookies, broken into coarse pieces

butter, for greasing

to serve

½ cup whipping cream

2 tbsp amaretto liqueur

1 oz/25 g semisweet chocolate, grated

method

1 Place the candied fruit, raisins, orange rind, and juice in a bowl and mix together. Put the light cream and chocolate in a pan and heat gently until the chocolate has melted. Stir until smooth, then stir in the fruit mixture. Let cool.

2 Lightly grease a 3½-cup ovenproof bowl with butter. Place the cream cheese and a little of the chocolate mixture in a large bowl and beat together until smooth, then stir in the remaining chocolate mixture. Stir in the broken amaretti cookies. Pour into the prepared bowl, cover with plastic wrap and let chill in the refrigerator overnight.

3 To serve, turn the pudding out onto a chilled serving plate. Pour the whipping cream into a bowl and add the amaretto liqueur. Whip lightly until slightly thickened. Pour some of the cream over the pudding and sprinkle grated chocolate over the top. Serve with the remaining cream.

mascarpone creams

ingredients

serves 4

4 oz/115 g amaretti cookies,
    crushed
1/4 cup amaretto or Maraschino
4 eggs, separated
generous 1/4 cup superfine sugar
1 cup mascarpone cheese
toasted slivered almonds,
    to decorate

method

1 Place the amaretti crumbs in a bowl, add the amaretto or Maraschino, and set aside to soak.

2 Meanwhile, beat the egg yolks with the superfine sugar until pale and thick. Fold in the mascarpone and soaked cookie crumbs.

3 Whisk the egg whites in a separate, spotlessly clean bowl until stiff, then gently fold into the cheese mixture. Divide the mascarpone cream among serving dishes and let chill for 1–2 hours. Sprinkle with toasted slivered almonds just before serving.

chilled chocolate dessert

ingredients

serves 4–6

1 cup mascarpone cheese
2 tbsp finely ground coffee beans
¼ cup confectioners' sugar
3 oz/85 g unsweetened
   chocolate, finely grated
1½ cups heavy cream, plus extra
   for decorating
Marsala, to serve

method

1 Beat the mascarpone with the coffee and confectioners' sugar until thoroughly combined.

2 Set aside 4 teaspoons of the grated chocolate and stir the remainder into the cheese mixture with 5 tablespoons of the unwhipped cream.

3 Whisk the remaining cream until it forms soft peaks. Stir 1 tablespoon of the cream into the mascarpone mixture to slacken it, then fold the cream into the remaining mascarpone mixture with a figure-eight action to blend it in.

4 Spoon the mixture into a freezerproof container and place in the freezer for about 3 hours.

5 To serve, scoop the chocolate dessert into sundae glasses and drizzle with a little Marsala. Top with the extra cream, whipped, and decorate with the reserved grated chocolate. Serve immediately.

cappuccino soufflé puddings

ingredients

serves 4

⅓ cup whipping cream
2 tsp instant espresso
    coffee granules
2 tbsp Kahlúa
3 large eggs, separated,
    plus 1 extra egg white
5½ oz/150 g semisweet chocolate,
    melted and cooled
2 tbsp golden superfine sugar,
    plus extra for coating
butter, for greasing
unsweetened cocoa, for dusting
vanilla ice cream or cookies,
    to serve

method

1 Lightly grease the sides of 4 x ¾-cup/175-ml ramekins with butter and coat with superfine sugar. Place the ramekins on a baking sheet.

2 Place the cream in a small, heavy-bottom pan and heat gently. Stir in the coffee until it has dissolved, then stir in the Kahlúa. Divide the coffee mixture between the prepared ramekins.

3 Place the egg whites in a clean, greasefree bowl and whisk until soft peaks form, then gradually whisk in the sugar until stiff but not dry. Stir the egg yolks and melted chocolate together in a separate bowl, then stir in a little of the whisked egg whites. Gradually fold in the remaining egg whites.

4 Divide the mixture among the dishes. Bake in a preheated oven, 375°F/190°C, for 15 minutes, or until just set. Dust with unsweetened cocoa and serve immediately with vanilla ice cream or cookies.

coffee panna cotta with chocolate sauce

ingredients

serves 6

oil, for brushing
2½ cups heavy cream
1 vanilla bean
generous ¼ cup golden superfine
    sugar
2 tsp instant espresso coffee
    granules, dissolved in
    ¼ cup water
2 tsp powdered gelatin

sauce
⅔ cup light cream
2 oz/55 g semisweet chocolate,
    melted

to decorate
chocolate-covered coffee beans
cocoa, for dusting

method

1 Lightly brush 6 x ⅔-cup/150-ml molds with oil. Place the cream in a pan. Split the vanilla bean and scrape the black seeds into the cream. Add the vanilla bean and the sugar, then heat gently until almost boiling. Strain the cream into a heatproof bowl and set aside. Place the coffee in a small heatproof bowl, sprinkle on the gelatin and let stand for 5 minutes, or until spongy. Set the bowl over a pan of gently simmering water until the gelatin has dissolved.

2 Stir a little of the reserved cream into the gelatin mixture, then stir the gelatin mixture into the remainder of the cream. Divide the mixture between the prepared molds and let cool, then let chill in the refrigerator for 8 hours, or overnight.

3 To make the sauce, place one-quarter of the cream in a bowl and stir in the melted chocolate. Gradually stir in the remaining cream, reserving 1 tablespoon. To serve the panna cotta, dip the base of the molds briefly into hot water and turn out onto six dessert plates. Pour the chocolate cream round. Dot drops of the reserved cream onto the sauce and feather it with a toothpick. Decorate with chocolate-covered coffee beans and cocoa. Serve immediately.

index